PRAISE FOR
DANCES WITH DOGS

"So, I get asked to endorse a lot of books. Thankfully, I finally learned to say no to most of these requests. But—holy smokes—am I ever thrilled I said 'yes' to this delightful offering from Bonnie Rose. *Dances with Dogs* is funny, profound, and well, it's a book I'd have read anyway. I loved learning more about this "irreverent reverend," and meeting the menagerie of pets and characters that inspired her epic spiritual adventure."

> —Pam Grout, #1 New York Times bestseller *of E-Squared, Thank and Grow Rich,* and 17 other books.

"As I write these words, outside my window a fire engine rushes past with sirens blaring, pushing peace and calm aside. I think back to the words I've just read in Bonnie Rose's book… 'through the power of paradox, inner hell becomes an invitation to practice heaven.' The book's words come to life. Written in a joyful and inspirational way, Bonnie shares her spiritual foundation though stories, insights, and reflections. She encourages us to see the world as whole, divine, and full of possibilities."

> — Kusala Bhikshu, Resident Zen/Thien Monk at International Buddhist Meditation Center, Los Angeles, CA.

"Bonnie puts her life on the page in a non-stuffy way that supports you in knowing you are so, so much more than ok—you are guided, loved, and an integral part of life. She defines herself as an "irreverent reverend". I say she's an everyday mystic just dancing with her dogs and teaching us all how to love, laugh and let go."

> — Rev. Mark Anthony Lord, Minister, Author, Relationship Coach.

"*Dances with Dogs* is a practical and fun guide for the modern seeker. In this book, you are sure to find helpful guidance for life's befuddlements—and cheerful companionship for your journey. Reverend Bonnie is honest, funny, and self-deprecating to the point that you cannot help but fall madly in love with her and take her advice straight to the heart of whatever may be troubling you."

—Rev. Dr. David Bruner

"*Dances with Dogs* is funny, strange, and surprising. Most of all, it is alive with joy. Reverend Bonnie's words remind us that, whenever possible, we can live with 'unbridled gratitude' for the ordinary and, in doing so, we might find the divine."

—Mandy Len Catron, Author of *How to Fall in Love with Anyone.*

DANCES
WITH DOGS

A Rowdy, Mystical Minister Shares
Memories of Human Comedy, Cosmic
Kindness, and Cat-Handling

REV. BONNIE ROSE

DANCES WITH DOGS
Published by Love-Dogs Publishing
First edition: June 2023

Copyright © 2023 by Bonnie Rose

All rights reserved. This book may not be reproduced in whole or in part, in any form (beyond copying permitted by Sections 107 and 108 of the United States Copyright Law, and except limited excerpts by reviewer for the public press), without written permission from Bonnie Rose.

This memoir is based on true stories. Some names are used with permission. Other names have been changed to protect privacy. Certain details have been adapted for story flow.

The information contained in this book is based on the experiences of the author and is to be used only for educational/inspirational purposes. This book is not a substitute for advice from licensed professionals. Those who wish to apply the ideas presented in this book are taking full responsibility for their actions.

Author photo: Gerard Burkhart

A portion of the proceeds from this book will be donated to charity.

Author services by Pedernales Publishing, LLC.
www.pedernalespublishing.com

Library of Congress Control Number: 2023906310

ISBN 979-8-9881104-7-7 Paperback Edition
     979-8-9881104-8-4 Hardcover Edition
     979-8-9881104-9-1 Digital Edition

Printed in the United States of America

For my friend Debbie.

"*Part of you pours out of me in these lines from time to time.*"
—Joni Mitchell

DANCES
WITH DOGS

CONTENTS

Introduction 3

Prologue 10

PART I: ON TOUR 17

    Ch. 1—The Cat had an Understudy? 19

    Ch. 2—The Ghastly Thread 23

    Ch. 3—The Laminatrix 28

    Ch. 4—Innocence 33

PART II: SLAM-DANCING IN CHURCH 39

    Ch. 5—Into the Chrysalis 41

    Ch. 6—Puppy-Mageddon 46

    Ch. 7—Befriending Failure 52

    Ch. 8—The Naked Burrito 59

    Ch. 9—The Mirror 65

    Ch. 10 —Unqualified 70

    Ch. 11—Chasing the Shadow 74

    Ch. 12—The Source of Shame 78

    Ch. 13—Loving the Shadow Into Light 85

    Ch. 14—Putting the Fun in Funeral 90

    Ch. 15—The Revenge of the Naked Burrito 94

PART III: DANCES WITH CANCER 99

    Ch. 16—Looking for Signs 101

    Ch. 17—The Day the Rabbit Died 106

    Ch. 18—The Cone of Shame 110

Ch. 19—Redefining Cancer 114

Ch. 20—The Purpose of Death 118

PART IV: PRICELESS 125

Ch. 21—Grasping and Grace 127

Ch. 22—Kindness 133

Ch. 23—Invincible and Invisible 136

Ch. 24—The Advances of Love 140

Ch. 25—Priceless 144

PART V: DANCING IN THE UNCONDITIONAL ABSOLUTE 151

Ch. 26—Licking the Law of Attraction 153

Ch. 27—The Holy Goat 157

Ch. 28—Freeing Senile Sacred Cows 163

Ch. 29—The Exultation of the Unconditional 169

Ch. 30—Who Licked the Vet? 175

PART VI: DANCES WITH SUFFERING AND JOY 179

Ch. 31—Know Nothing, Trust Everything 181

Ch. 32—Prayers on a Plane 186

Ch. 33—Holding On and Letting Go 192

Ch. 34—Vulnerability - Blessing or Curse? 195

Ch. 35—Suffering is the New Joy 200

Ch. 36—Requiem for a Dog 205

Ch. 37—Tears at a Tea Party 209

Ch. 38—Love and Loss 214

PART VII: FROM GRIEF TO GRATITUDE 217

    Ch. 39—Om Saraswati 219

    Ch. 40—The Sound of Wings 225

    Ch. 41—The Whole World is One Family 228

    Ch. 42—Then is Now and There is Here 236

PART VIII: GLOBAL KINDNESS 241

    Ch. 43—Back to India 243

    Ch. 44—Silent Bows 247

    Ch. 45—Unconditional Success 253

    Ch. 46—Buddhists Gone Wild 259

    Ch. 47—Kindness Around the World 262

    Ch. 48—Compassion Consciousness 269

Epilogue: The Circle Game 275

Acknowledgments 281

Endnotes 284

Four sisters and a dog--Nancy, Judy, Jinx, Bonnie, and Carol.

INTRODUCTION

"Open my eyes that I may see."
—Hymn by Clara Scott

When I was a child in the 1960s, most of my friends played with Barbie dolls. I played with a skeleton. My sisters and I named her Bessie the Skel.

Judy, my eldest sister, gave Bessie to me for my birthday. Made out of cream-colored plastic, Bessie was about the same size as a Barbie doll, minus the enormous breasts. Like Barbie, Bessie had a couture wardrobe, a cardboard dream house, and a pink convertible car. She had two yarn wigs for her bony head—one yellow and one black. There was no Ken equivalent, but Bessie didn't care. She was a forerunner to feminism—an avant-garde skinnier version of Twiggy.

My parents had four daughters, first Judy, then Nancy. Carol was born six years after Nancy, and then I came along. Nancy was often busy with her teenage friends, but Judy loved to design games for her littlest sisters. Judy dressed us in pirate costumes with black polyester pants, over-sized white shirts, and tin foil hooks for hands. Our pirate capes were re-purposed beach towels, and we carried a black-and-white skull and crossbones flag, crafted by Judy on our mother's vintage Singer sewing machine. On pirate days, we swash-buckled to our backyard flagpole and raised up our Jolly Roger to warn the neighbors about the impending pirate invasion of our lush Manhattan suburb.

One of Judy's best games was called "blind school." Today, this game probably would not glide through the sphincter of political correctness, but Judy had empathy for those who couldn't see and taught us to appreciate our own vision. Judy's games were never mean-spirited, and blind school was not about appropriating sightless people. Rather, Judy recognized how the sighted take the gift of seeing for granted. She designed an experience to give us empathy and a new perspective on life.

Blind school came into session when Judy told us tales of blind children in special schools where they learned to navigate the world. Then she blindfolded Carol and me with our mother's Betty Crocker-style aprons. Once the aprons were fastened over our eyes, Judy prompted us to go through an obstacle course comprised of cinderblock-sized red cardboard bricks spread across our living room floor. Carol and I walked with arms outstretched from one end of the living room to the other, staggering into floral wing chairs and tripping over bricks. Our cheerful black terrier-mix, Jinx, assumed the role of bumbling seeing-eye dog. Jinx pranced beside us and tangled our ankles in her silver chain leash.

At blind school lunchtime, Judy pointed us toward the kitchen. We held hands and let Jinx lead us on a meandering grope to the breakfast nook. Once we arrived, Judy propped us on the benches around our kitchen table. There she placed Franciscan Apple dinnerware plates in front of us, each holding 10 to 15 mini-marshmallows.

"Your plate is like a clock," she said. "You have food at 3 o'clock and 7 o'clock."

She gave us forks and told us to eat. "Use your forks, not your fingers," she instructed. Clad in early 1960's Dacron-polyester with aprons on our heads, Carol and I stabbed at frisky mini-marshmallows that evaded capture while our big sister looked on, merrily devising her next scheme.

There is a point to this…

The words of a Jewish prayer tell us "We walk sightless among miracles."[1] In the Gospel of Thomas, Jesus says, "The kingdom of heaven is spread upon the earth, but we do not see it."[2] We fail to see the amazing goodness of God in all things. As we navigate the miracle of being alive, we trip over bricks, stab at objects, get tangled in imaginary chains, and we ask ourselves: *What is going on here? Why is life against us? What is wrong with me?*

Life is not against us and there is nothing wrong with you. We are simply blind to the truth, blinded by the metaphorical aprons over our eyes. In absolute reality—a reality *unaffected by the beliefs or limitations of any finite being*—the grace of God is always present.

Mystical teachers define heaven and hell not as literal post-mortem destinations, but as states of mind. In mental hell, we sweat in the flames of shame, guilt, and hatefulness. We focus on what is wrong with life. In mental heaven, we behold God's omnipresent miracles. We know all beings are worthy of love, and we delight in the joy of sacred service.

Because we have been blessed by free will, we can *choose* to be in heaven or hell here on earth at any moment. If we impose our bounded perspectives on boundless reality—if we criticize ourselves and judge others—we experience inner hell. If we release our narrow-minded "hellish" perspectives and open ourselves to a divine point of view, we awaken to the consciousness of heaven.

---

1   From a Jewish Sabbath Prayer: "Days pass, years vanish, and we walk sightless among miracles."
2   The Gospel of Thomas, Saying 113.

The consciousness of heaven is grace, joy, love, learning, service, and so much more. The consciousness of heaven is infinite and eternal. It is non-dual, meaning beyond opposites and inclusive of everything. It is limitless, only *seemingly* limited by individual awareness. And here's the most amazing news: life can be glorious all the time, because through the power of paradox, inner hell becomes an invitation to *practice* heaven.

The practice of heaven on earth is a back-and-forth process. We behold and backslide. At times we languish in despair, but then grace surprises us in strange places. We undergo infinite cycles of lurching, searching, finding, forgetting, and back again.

In my job as a minister, when I give my Sunday sermons, I often speak about the kingdom of heaven on earth, what it means, and how it exists everywhere—here and now. For a few moments, the congregation and I align with the wonders of the divine. But after service, I forget. By the time I get in the car to go home, I am usually preoccupied with other details. I zip past the glistening Pacific Ocean without noticing. My route takes me through our local orchard groves where I ignore the gift of fruit growing. I skip over God's majesty before me, blinded by mundane distractions. I stress about how life refuses to unfold according to *my* plans. I compartmentalize grace as if to say, *This situation in my life is heaven, this one is hell. Let me worry about the hellish one until I "fix" it.*

But some days I awaken in my car and say to myself, *Wait, did you hear what you said in church this morning? Heaven is here and now. Open the "eyes of your eyes!"*[3] *See if you can shift your perspective. Look through the lens of wholeness.*

When I arrive home, I climb out of my turquoise Prius and glance at the front yard. There, my husband tenderly prunes our yellow roses. He clips the bushes down to bare nubs, trusting

---

3   From a poem by e.e. cummings: *i thank You God for most this amazing.* The quote is "now the eyes of my eyes are opened."

the kingdom of nature to restore them in the spring. I look beyond my husband to the mountains in the distance, pinkish in the fading light. Here, I imagine another realm of heaven—chattering squirrels and fierce mountain lions sequestered in the sunset, each immersed in the art of being. The next day I go for a pedicure where Henri, a balding Vietnamese gentleman, kneels before me as I sit in a cracked brown leather recliner. I test the footbath temperature with my big toe. Henri frowns when he sees my brick-like calluses cemented from miles of hiking in the mountains with our dogs—and I silently say, *Henri, bless your bald head. Thank you for nurturing my feet*—for the kingdom of heaven is in Henri, too.

In moments like these, I celebrate the hidden wholeness of God. I see the beloved in the squirrels, in the calluses, in the decapitated roses. This presence is gentle, unsightly, wild, infinite, and intimate. I trust the divine in every detail of creation—known and unknown. It is in me, in my fear, my doubt, my forgetfulness, and my tenure in blind school because all these things inspire deeper awakening. And I say to myself, *Thank you, Divine Love. Thank you, God. Thank you for dissolving my distractions. Thank you for illuminating your outrageous holiness. Thank you for restoring me to insanity—the madness of a dervish whirl of wonder.*

With a little dedication and joy, we *all* can awaken to the holiness spread upon the earth in every detail of our lives.

In the spirit of unbridled gratitude, I share my stories in this book, laden with the good, the bad, and the in between, knowing it is all miraculous. This is not a self-help book, and I don't claim to have the answers to life's mysteries. But I do know when I court these principles with joy, I remember everything belongs, and I trust life can be good for all.

I share my journey—my moments of awakening to spirit and my tendency to fall asleep. I write about the days I trust God completely—as well as the days when I can't pray myself out of a paper bag. I tell the tale of a life fiercely woven together in a seamless robe of cosmic glory and comedic minutia. And although these chapters seem to be about the details of *my* life, it's really a story about all of us. I trust my words will lead us to a place where we remember "the uses of adversity are sweet," and there is "good in everything."[4] God in everything. Love in everything.

A few warnings: I use various terms for God—the divine, beloved, love, source, absolute reality, life, the infinite, and more. If you don't like what I call this un-nameable energy, just translate. Call it whatever feels right to you. Call it Louise, if that makes you happy.

There are also gender issues. Some folks may react if I refer to heaven as a kingdom, thinking it implies patriarchy. Others will be offended by the use of feminine pronouns for God. We don't really need to worry about any of that. God is beyond gender.

Others struggle with the word "heaven." Think of it as grace, non-dual consciousness, the mystery beyond opposites, abundance, worthiness, acceptance, love, beauty, or any good word that works for you. Remember mere words are fingers pointing at the moon. It's best to focus on the moon, not the finger. That means focus on the cosmic principles, not our dearly inadequate attempts to describe the mysteries of absolute reality.[5]

---

4 "Sweet are the uses of adversity" and "Good in everything" are quotes from *As You Like It,* by William Shakespeare. The full quote is: "Sweet are the uses of adversity, which like the toad, ugly and venomous, wears yet a precious jewel in his head; and this our life, exempt from public haunt, finds tongues in trees, books in the running brooks, sermons in stones, and good in everything. I would not change it.."

5 There are many versions of the "finger pointing at the moon" quote. One is, "The finger is needed to know where to look for the moon, but if you mistake the finger for the moon itself, you will never know the real moon." Thich Nhat Hanh, *Old Path White Clouds: Walking in the Footsteps of the Buddha* (Berkeley: Parallax Press, 1991).

I also write about my imperfections. Many see flaws as unspiritual, but I have found my imperfections are perfect teachers. I expose my allegedly unspiritual spots to offer insight. Luckily, I'm like a Dalmatian. I have a ton of spots I shamelessly reveal for our shared growth and understanding. You're welcome.

I provide key points at the end of each story for thought, prayer, and action. These suggestions invite us to use our heads, hearts, and hands to personalize the concepts I share. Please feel free to embrace, adapt, or abandon my suggestions to meet your own needs and preferences.

Lastly, I tend to be irreverent. The "Irreverent Reverend" they call me. My irreverence springs from delight in the holy human comedy. I find a willingness to laugh disarms judgment. Some find my irreverent joy problematic. So if you're easily offended, maybe stay away from the chapter about licking the veterinarian. If you're opposed to profanity, steer clear of the section where I come down with a case of cancer. If you're dainty, you may want to avoid the part about the cashier and his naked burrito.

If, however, you are open to seeing God's grace everywhere; if you choose to celebrate the entire spectrum of sacred, mundane, and profane as one; if you're intrigued by the paradox of being a human held in the divine—or the divine held in a human—then read on. Know through these words, the human-divine in me celebrates the human-divine in you.

My hope in sharing these stories is to help us collectively graduate from blind school and rewrite that saying from the Gospel of Thomas: *The kingdom of heaven is spread upon the earth. May we see it, be it, live it, and love it, as it is, in everything—including ourselves.*

Namaste.[6]

---

[6] Namaste means "I bow to you." It is a way of honoring the divinity in another.

PROLOGUE: DANCES WITH DOGS

> "When it's over, I want to say: all my life I was a bride married to amazement. I was the bridegroom, taking the world into my arms."
>
> —Mary Oliver

What is the kingdom of heaven?

I was raised to believe the kingdom of heaven is an afterlife destination-spa, a place where we get to go when we die *if* we have behaved and believed. Later I learned a mystical interpretation of Jesus's words. The kingdom of heaven is about presence and immediacy. "The kingdom of God is within you" (Luke 21:17); "the kingdom of heaven is at hand" (Matthew 3:2). The realm of heaven is here and now, waiting to be received and experienced. Again, heaven is a state of mind, a way of being in the world—but "not of the world" (John 17:16). The kingdom of heaven is a name for an ever-available shift into non-dual consciousness. It is awareness of an absolute reality that transcends the either/or thinking of the small egoic self. The kingdom of heaven includes everything given and received in a *Möbius* strip of ongoing goodness.[7]

If the kingdom of heaven is present, why can't we see it? Why do we walk sightless among miracles?

We have an ego, an aspect of being we call the separate self. The ego helps us navigate life. It helps us load the dishwasher, floss our teeth, and pay our bills. It encourages us to drive on the proper side of the road and prevents klutzes like me from bungee jumping. As the ego helps us define safe boundaries, it provides comfort. The ego is a good thing because it engenders our survival, but it has limitations. The ego is literal and lacks the capacity to see the shades of grey essential to mystical thinking.

Mystical author Cynthia Bourgeault calls the ego "the binary operating system." She writes our brains are like a computer and "our pre-installed binary system runs on the power of 'either/or.' This dualistic 'binary operator' is built right into the structure of the human brain…"[i]

The binary operating system of the brain seeks patterns to help us understand our surroundings. In a way, the ego is like a student at blind school. It needs predictable roadmaps. It needs to know the locations of the large cardboard bricks that threaten to trip us. The ego finds peace when it knows our blind school food rests on a plate precisely at 3 o'clock and 7 o'clock. However, when life's conditions inevitably shift, the ego feels threatened, so it projects its static patterns onto a dynamic world. This ego-strategy often traps us in a shrunken reality of our own making.

---

7   A Möbius strip is often used as a symbol of infinity. Google's English Dictionary defines it as "a surface with one continuous side formed by joining the ends of a rectangular strip after twisting one end 180 degrees." It's like a figure 8 with a twist. So when you trace the surface of a Möbius strip with your finger, you move from inside to outside without breaking contact. If you google it and find a picture, the visual will make it clearer than words.

The comfort of ego patterns came alive for me one day at the height of the COVID-19 pandemic. I had time on my hands, so I purged our closets and hefted three bulging boxes of discarded items to Goodwill. The volunteer in charge of receiving donations was apologetic as he said, "We have new COVID policies. You'll need to sort the clothes, books, and housewares into these blue bins all by yourself. I'm not allowed to help. I hope that's okay."

"Are you kidding me?" I told him. "That's the best news I've had in months." My ego was ecstatic.

In a pandemic fraught with uncertainty, I was aching for control. It was electrifying to establish order and put everything in its proper place. *If only the rest of my life was so well-defined*, I thought to myself, as I tossed my painful patent leather pumps into the clothing bin. *If only I could sort the chaos of unanswered questions COVID-19 inspires, such as how will this virus change life on the planet earth? When will this stinker-of-a-pandemic be done? Who will live and who will die?*

The ego likes to sort. It feels secure when it can say, *This is good, but this is evil; this is joyful, but this is sorrowful; this is something I can love, but this other thing goes in the hate bin.* The ego places humans in sorting bins saying, *This person is forgivable, but this one is not*; or, *Today I am loveable, but yesterday I was unworthy.* Again, the ego struggles with uncertainty, ambiguity, and shades of grey. The ego likes patterns. So every day and always, we squeeze the infinite into known and manageable sorting bins. When we do this, we fail to see the kingdom of heaven on earth. We become blind to God's grace in *all* things.

Is there an alternative way of being?

The universe is too magnificent to sort. When it's time for us to evolve spiritually, God nudges us and invites us to let go. Then, if we wake up with fresh eyes, present to life's treasures—even treasures in challenges—we embark upon a path of understanding beyond knowing. We experience a shift in consciousness. Led by trust, we tiptoe toward an inner space where we set aside our sorting bins. We inhabit a creative field of wholeness that infuses all life.

Now, many of us are caught in a belief that bigger is better. Because of this misperception, we often believe the treasures of heaven should sort into containers labeled vast and grand, such as pearly gates and streets of gold. But we don't have to postpone heaven on earth until life is bigger and better. Heaven on earth exists in tiny, simple spaces, too. Abundant treasures wait for us, camouflaged by the ordinary.

In the early 1990s, my husband, Hugh, and I lived in New York. One night, we attended an off-Broadway show called *The Boys Next Door*, by Tom Griffin. It's a serious comedy about people who live in a group home for adults who are differently-abled. This play offers the audience a thoughtful perspective on the home residents and their caregivers. It allows us to find beauty in the wide spectrum of human conditions.

I remember one staggering scene in this play. The residents of the group home attend a social gathering in a gym. This is *not* the dance in the gym scene from *West Side Story*. There are no gorgeous gang members doing flirty choreography, no potential for turf warfare. In this scene, two residents, Norman and Sheila, shuffle over to each other. Norman is overweight, wearing mismatched plaids. His pants are pulled up above his waist, leaving a wide expanse of white socks at the cuff. Shelia is pudgy with slumped posture. She has a protruding middle and wears a thrift store tweed skirt with a fussy, yellow ruffled blouse, partially untucked. They speak to each other abruptly, without nuance or grace. They blurt out well-meaning comments but say the wrong things. They overshare. You can tell they like each other and soon they begin a slow, lumbering dance out of time with the music.

Suddenly, the music becomes louder and the lights become softer. The audience enters a dream state with Norman and Sheila. We enter *their* reality where they are not their bodies and not their simple minds. They are smitten, and their love makes them glamorous. They glow as they gaze into each other's eyes. They become a modern-day Fred and Ginger as their simple movements soar and their inner beauty dissolves outer disabilities.

This moment lasted only 10 seconds, but my husband and I both sobbed out loud in the theater. I still cry when I think of it. Because sometimes, for an instant, I'm Norman and Sheila. Sometimes, my inner lights change, and I find grace in my ordinary life.

It happens when I dance with my dogs. We have two Hungarian Vizslas, big red-haired, muscular, high-energy pointers. Both are treat-hounds, and by that, I mean treat-harlots. They willingly endure the indignities I impose upon them, all for a scrap of kibble.

Often, when I should be doing something grown-up, I play a recording of an accordion solo, "The Julida Polka." I wear an oversized pink *Life is Good* hoodie and decrepit black-and-white polka dot pajama bottoms that sag at the knees. I fill my pockets with kibble and corral the dogs. The treats inspire them to perform hit-or-miss choreography. I command rapid sits and down-stays. We lope through a polka figure eight. Our older dog wanders off to harass our cat, and the puppy pauses to yelp at a fragment of kibble that rolled under the couch. I bellow at them to come back and pay attention, and we keep dancing.

My overachieving arts-oriented family visited one day, and the dogs and I performed the dance for them. My nephew glanced up from texting and said, "It needs work." He's right, it does. The dance is pathetic, but I don't mind. On a good day, we dance imperfectly for hours. Hours.

I'm the senior minister of a church. There are sermons to write, interfaith activities to plan, and hospital visits to attend. Weddings, funerals, and fundraisers tug at me. I have a life outside the church, a husband, and 20-plus animals. I need to do something about the pet-hair-toupee sprouting on the living room rug. I should fill in our rabbit's garden-excavation-project and vanquish the poop pile-up in the backyard. Yet, the polka beckons.

The dance may be an elaborate procrastination strategy, something to help me avoid the treachery of responsibilities I fear and face daily, something to keep me from inhabiting my life fully. It is. But then there is a place in our polka. A place where the music changes.

We hear an accordion fanfare and I coax the dogs to parade around me in a slow circle. In my mind, the lights dim, the room becomes hazy, and I'm in a dream. I'm Norman and Sheila in that scene from *The Boys Next Door*, an imagined (or is it real) version of myself. I am a circus performer with a dancer's posture. I'm wearing a sparkling pointy bra, red patent leather cowboy boots, and a gold sequined crinoline. I have a stunning command of the animal kingdom, my two Vizsla-lions. As I turn, I smile at the imagined audience. The dogs cooperate, and for a moment, I am accomplished. I am significant. I am bold.

It occurs to me I may also be delusional. But probably not. Because when I'm 99 or so, when the dogs are long gone; when I have three teeth left and I'm living on grey vegan puree; when I'm wearing adult diapers…maybe I'll look back if my mind is clear enough to do so. Sure, I'll remember the accomplishments of my life—the answered prayers, the music, the mystery, the church that changed lives. But I hope I remember most my clumsy dance with the dogs—my clumsy dance with all creation—like it's the holiest thing on earth. Because it is.

Reflections

Head: What is the holiest thing on earth for you? What simple moments bring you deep love, joy, peace, or well-being?

Heart: Divine Love, show me magnificence in the ordinary moments of my life.

Hands: Put aside your to-do list. Do something simple to open your heart to holiness.

PART ONE: ON TOUR

THE CAT HAD AN UNDERSTUDY?

"I dwell in possibility."
—Emily Dickenson

When people interview me for spiritual speaker events, podcasts, or radio shows, the host usually asks about my history to provide context. The conversation goes something like this:

Host: Reverend Bonnie, tell us about yourself.

Bonnie: Well, I was born in New York. I moved to North Carolina to go to college, first to Duke for a degree in nursing, and then to North Carolina School of the Arts where I got a degree in opera. I moved back to New York where I worked as a nurse, opera singer, and actress. I sang in a bunch of operas and did choral work. I married my husband, Hugh, who is an actor and a spiritual seeker. I was an understudy in *Shadowlands*, a Broadway show about the Christian author, C.S. Lewis. I was also part of the Broadway tour of *Lettice and Lovage*, a play by Peter Shaffer. Julie Harris was the star. I had a small role, plus the play had a live cat onstage so I handled the cat and the cat's understudy.

After the play, we moved to California where I worked some more in opera and nursing. During that time, I became active in a church. Eventually I went to ministerial school then became a part-time staff minister. Then I got a job as the senior minister of a church—The Ventura Center for Spiritual Living. It's been a fantastic journey and we've built a wonderful church dedicated to love. I'm also involved in an organization called ServiceSpace that promotes global kindness—and here I am today.

Host: What an interesting journey…but jump back to the part about the Broadway tour. The cat had an understudy…?

The kingdom of heaven on earth has many mansions for us to explore. Discovering God's reality means awakening to mansions of possibility. Prior to 1992, I never imagined I would someday handle a cat and her understudy in a Broadway tour, but the realm of possibility ushered me in a new direction.

I always liked animals. We had many pets when I was a child. When I first started singing professionally, I swore off pets, thinking I needed to focus on my career. Then Hugh got me a cat for Christmas. She was a Chinchilla Silver Persian with huge green eyes. We named her Miranda, based on the character in Shakespeare's *The Tempest*.

I fell madly in love with Miranda, the seer of human souls and the ruination of my life. My interest in a singing career dwindled as I became obsessed with our cat. Wherever I went, whether it was a 12-hour nursing shift, an audition, or life on the road for a show, I felt a cat magnet pulling me home.

When I lived in New York, all the aspiring singers and actors read *Backstage Magazine* for audition listings. One day, I picked up a copy and saw there was a national Broadway tour of *Lettice and Lovage*, a British comedy by Peter Shaffer, who is probably best known for writing *Amadeus* and *Equus*. Julie Harris, a renowned actress of stage and screen, was to play the title role of Lettice Douffet.

I read the cast list and saw there was a role for Hugh. British comedy is one of his fortes. There were a bunch of smaller parts for men and women, and technically, I had the skills to perform one of them. I had understudied on Broadway, so I had my Equity card, and I was stage savvy from singing opera. I didn't have the years of regional theater, Shakespeare, and Broadway credits I knew the thousands of other actors vying for these parts would have. But I had a cat. There was a role for a live cat onstage. The spirit of possibility awakened in me, and I knew I wanted to go for this. If we got cast, we could do a high-end Broadway tour on a family plan. Hugh was excited about the possibility, too.

I took the subway to Manhattan to purchase a copy of the play. I devoured it on the train ride home and plummeted as I read about the cat's role. If we got cast, Miranda would be on stage for about 10 minutes. She would have to tolerate screaming, doorbell ringing, running, and door pounding. Granted, she would be held by Julie Harris the whole time, but pretty much, the cat needed the personality of a sofa cushion. This was dicey. It was not Miranda. She could become a flailing demon when she didn't get her way. She once gouged our vet's artery with her talons, and the groomers at the Pretty Kitty Salon in Brooklyn took cover when they saw her coming.

Could Miranda do this role? We didn't know, so we took her for a test drive. We called our landlady, aptly named Mrs. Fish, to come downstairs for a visit or potential cat-mauling. We pried Miranda from behind the couch and placed her in Mrs. Fish's arms. Miranda squiggled and scratched her way to freedom and scampered into the bedroom. I looked at Hugh and said, "Our family plan. Our huge paycheck. Gone. Under the bed."

Yet, possibility prevailed—this time with spiritual work. The Law of Attraction, made famous by the book/movie *The Secret*, was not universally known yet. But Hugh read *Think and Grow*

Rich, by Napoleon Hill, and I read *You Can Heal Your Life*, by Louise Hay. The basic premise of this work is you can attract what you want into your life by changing your thinking. You can manifest positive results through the power of your thoughts.

We applied Law of Attraction principles to our cat and our future. We meditated on success. We visualized touring as a family. We hired a cat psychiatrist who made house calls.

At the risk of sounding judgmental, let's just say someone who aspires to be a cat psychiatrist might be a few grains shy of a full litter box. We gave it a try anyway. The cat psychiatrist, a small grey-haired man, arrived at our front door wearing a pale blue polyester leisure suit. We brought him into our living room, where Miranda expressed her disgust by looking away and sharpening her claws on the arm of an easy chair. The cat psychiatrist was nonplussed. He didn't have the patient lie on a tiny couch and meow about her mother and/or her abandonment issues. Rather, he interviewed the humans in the room. At the end of the session, he made us a tape of cat affirmations, a continuous loop to play every day.

Hugh went to Pittsburgh to star in the play, *Noises Off*. I stayed home alone and listened to hours of affirmations: "Miranda is a calm kitty…Miranda is a kind kitty…Miranda is a gentle kitty."

I wasn't sure if Miranda would ever be a calm kitty. But I *was* sure I was about ready to stick a pencil in my eye.

Reflections

Head: What is your "impossible" dream?

Heart: Divine Love, replace my possibilities with God's possibilities.

Hands: Take one tiny step toward the allegedly impossible. Then another.…

THE GHASTLY THREAD

"Trust in God but tether your camel too."
—Arab Proverb

The cat psychiatrist was legit. The cat affirmations seemed to rub off, maybe on Miranda, but also on me. When it came time to contact the casting people, I was a calm kitty. They rejected me at first, telling me I wasn't experienced enough to manage cat travel. For a moment, I experienced the mental hell of disappointment. But hell exists to awaken us to the possibility of heaven. In this case, I called forth heaven on earth though prayer plus action.

My prayerful mind drifted to my work as a registered nurse. Nurses anticipate complications and plan for solutions in advance. I realized I could merge nurse-mind with actor-cat-lover mind. *You were made for this,* I told myself. *You are the one who can keep the show cat safe through the complexities of acting and touring.*

I researched airlines and created a spreadsheet to define in-flight requirements for animals. I gave it to the company manager and said, "You can have this document whether you hire me or not." They liked my spreadsheet, and I was back in the running.

Then the director complained Miranda was not an officially trained stage cat. I prayed again. The prayer inspired me to make a collage of photos to showcase Miranda's charismatic beauty. The casting people liked it, but told us they might go with another actor for *my* role. I prayed and spewed out their objections like a hairball.

"Does this other actor have a cat?" I asked. "Does she have a spreadsheet?"

Finally, the casting people agreed to meet with us.

Hugh got cast in a small part and as an understudy for two leads who had already been determined. A few days later, Miranda the cat took a meeting with the director, Michael Blakemore, the author, Peter Shaffer, and the star, Julie Harris. I met them, too, as a potential cat handler and actor, but mostly as an afterthought.

Miranda and I rode the elevator up to the audition space. I whispered the cat affirmations, hoping they would hold up for both of us. Once inside the audition studio, I chatted with the casting people. I held our silver-white cat with one hand against my turquoise jacket. Miranda snuggled against me like a teddy bear. Julie Harris also held Miranda, who purred to prove she was indeed a calm kitty. The casting folks liked both of us. They hired Miranda and said I would be her handler. I would also perform onstage in one of the small roles.

Then another wrinkle: a day later, they decided Miranda was too beautiful for the role. When I objected, they said Miranda could be the understudy, but if we wanted the job, I had to find a scruffier cat.

Again, more prayer and focused action. We went on a cat hunt and found Fiona, a brown tabby. Her human mom was Suzy, the owner of a high-end cat accessory store in the upper east side of Manhattan. Fiona was exceedingly friendly. She was a natural, an authentically calm kitty. Suzy's children had grown up and moved away, and Fiona was lonely at home by herself. Suzy felt donating Fiona's services to a Broadway tour would help the kitty get the love and attention she craved. We took another meeting with the power people, this time with Fiona.

Later, Hugh's agent called.

"I don't know how you did it," he said.

"What do you mean?" Hugh asked.

"You got the job. You pulled this thing out the ethers. High-end Broadway tours with roles for a husband, a wife, and two cats do not grow on trees."

How did we do it? How did we pull this job out of the ethers? We got this job because we followed the teachings of an Arab proverb: *Trust in God but tether your camel too.*

We had many anxious nail-biting moments. The process was excruciating at times. When our faith faltered, we often succumbed to fear and imagined we would never achieve our goal. At one point, Hugh mournfully told his agent, "We're hanging by a ghastly thread."

The ghastly thread was a symbol of our fear—fear of disappointment, rejection, failure, and uncertainty—the things that plague most of us in one way or another. Eventually, we found a way to work with fear, instead of allowing fear to work against us. Over and over again, Hugh and I used spiritual practices to detangle ourselves from the snare of the ghastly thread.

Prayer helped us transform fear to faith. We noticed how the fearful ego tried to warn us of inevitable failure and disappointment. Investing our energy in these dire tales would have kept us safe, yet frustrated in the status quo. So we transcended the inner voices that urged us to abandon hope, and we prayed for new possibilities. Prayers for the possible anchored us in courageous vulnerability—a place where we could be still (between tantrums of self-doubt) and wait for God's plan.

The waiting was fingernails-on-a-blackboard-awful at times. But in this deeply uncomfortable state of limbo, we discovered answered prayers rarely arrive all at once. Prayer-results do not present themselves in large, gift-wrapped boxes, accompanied by a blaze of trumpets. Answered prayers usually arrive in bite-sized tidbits of tenuous grace. The result of prayer is not a prize—prayer is a *process*—a process of *gradual* shifts in consciousness as we learn to relax, trust life, and receive.

Our answered prayers were almost always incremental inspirations to "tether our camel too." In other words, to add hands and feet to our prayers; to do the next right thing in the world of form; to turn anxiety into action by taking small, sometimes ridiculous steps, toward fulfillment. Loving prayer became loving action, and this kept us moving "in the direction of our dreams."[8]

In fact, the whole process of "pulling a Broadway tour out of the ethers" was fueled by love. Love transcended the snare of the ghastly thread. Love gave us the stamina and courage to persist when things seemed impossible. Love for each other, love of the theater, and love for our dear cats coaxed us toward a new reality. A Broadway tour on a family plan was exactly what we needed to magnify and multiply love. And this was a good thing—because love *always* wants to magnify and multiply through all of us.

---

[8] A quote by Henry David Thoreau: "Go confidently in the direction of your dreams! Live the life you've imagined."

Bonnie and Hugh in costume, Lettice and Lovage National Tour.

Reflections

Head: What do you love? What "ghastly thread" threatens to keep you from a fuller expression of your love?

Heart: Divine Love, encourage me to magnify and multiply love.

Hands: Trust in God and tether your camel too. Take small, sometimes ridiculous action steps in the world of form. Trust the process and notice your answered prayer arriving in "bite-sized tidbits of tenuous grace."

THE LAMINATRIX

"You discover that your longings are universal longings, that you're not lonely and isolated from anyone. You belong."

— F. Scott Fitzgerald.

So we got cast in the Broadway tour, all four of us. Now I had to do something about it.

There is a hazard to getting what you pray for. You realize you are completely unprepared. Heaven on earth doesn't call the qualified; heaven qualifies the called. God offers on-the-job training. We're not ready to do what we're inspired to do until we've done it. I didn't know all this until years later. So when we got cast in the show, even though I wanted it, I unabashedly freaked out.

I anticipated feeling like an outcast. I imagined my new colleagues and trembled in the face of their collective expertise. I imagined them chatting learnedly about the merits of Shakespeare while I interjected best strategies for scraping boogers out of the cats' eyes. Like I said, I had been onstage before, but mostly in operas. I feared I would be seen as an unsophisticated rube compared to everyone else—someone who hadn't earned her place at the table.

And the cat handling, what was I thinking? Granted, I had that spreadsheet about airlines. I read a few books about cat care. I purchased a cat food cookbook that encouraged cat guardians to simulate the innards of a dead mouse in our meal preparation. I could clip nails in a pinch, and with a little determination, wrestle the cats into their carriers. But did I really know how to manage the challenges of a cat onstage in a complex scene with a celebrity? I was sure the higher-ups in the company would discover I was an imposter. Because I was. Totally faking it.

In the meantime, the cats were calm and rather disdainful about it all, especially Grandma. (We changed the "star" cat's name from Fiona to Grandma.) Grandma was elderly and the name seemed to fit. She liked her new name. In fact, she enjoyed everything about her life.

Grandma slept her way to the top. Literally. Twenty hours a day. She slept on the subway from Brooklyn to Manhattan on our way to rehearsal. In the rehearsal studio, she slept in her carrier. When her scene came up, she'd act for a while, get some notes from the director, receive love from the cast, then yawn, stretch, lick her bottom, and meander back into her bed-cave to sleep some more.

Grandma was unflappable, so I decided to adopt her as my role model. I didn't exactly sleep my way to the top unless you want to count my husband. I didn't lick my own bottom. I reassured myself how my acting scenes in this play were easier than singing opera. I could relax. I had one line: "Good heavens." And while it's *possible* to mess up "good heavens"—I know this because I did mess it up once—the rest of the time I bellowed my line with pristine elocution, perfectly timed in response to Julie Harris's cue. Changing my thinking around the ease of my acting role gave me an inch of confidence.

Still, I was insecure, particularly in the role of cat handler. I waited for someone to discover my lack of qualifications and push the eject button.

Then, again through a combination of prayer, action, and destiny, I awakened to heaven-consciousness and became indispensable.

We finished rehearsals in Manhattan and drove to New Haven for previews. The next step was our first airline flight. We would travel to Toronto for opening night. I learned getting animals across the Canadian border could be problematic, so I met with the company manager to discuss logistics. He twitched his fingers and his eyes darted from the flight schedule to my incompetent face.

"Do you have the papers for the cats?" He asked with a scowl, referring to the rabies and health certificates required for international travel.

"I have three sets of all the papers," I replied. "I'll carry the originals in my purse and will attach copies to their in-flight under-the-seat carriers. I will place a third copy on their airport/ground transportation carriers. And, by the way, I had everything laminated."

I saw the company manager's body relax. His pupils dilated in a rush of respect and that was it. My nurse-like anal retentive zeal paid off. Somehow, the approval I received from the company manager awakened the perception of my importance to this tour. I knew I belonged. I had something to offer. I was a Laminatrix.

When we're fully aware of our divine nature, we don't need approval from others to determine our right to belong. At the beginning of the tour, I craved validation. I still sometimes look to others to validate my worth. The need to feel good, welcomed, and whole is universal. We all long to belong.

But the *fulfillment* of our "belonging" springs from within. It is our nature to belong here and now, no matter what. We all belong to life. We cannot be cast out or separate. Separation is an illusion designed by the false self—an illusion designed by an illusion. And our yearning to belong is *not* about absence. It is about presence—a vague and veiled remembrance of our place, not only *in* eternal presence, but *as* eternal presence.

We seek what we already have. We are like the sun seeking the sun. Sometimes clouds block the rays of the sun, but the sun keeps shining. Sometimes clouds of illusion overshadow our true nature. But beyond the clouds, our divine nature shines eternally. Everyone is holy and everyone belongs. Even our forgetfulness belongs—because forgetfulness amplifies remembrance.

How do we remember our place as eternal presence when we feel separate? How do we know wherever we are, we are already home, holy, and whole?

It's ironic to me that my one-line (my monologue I like to call it) in this miraculously acquired play was two words: "Good heavens!" Perhaps my monologue functioned like an affirmation, said eight times a week under the hot stage lights in the presence of witnesses—the other cast members and the audience. Perhaps I started to believe my monologue and live like the truth of omnipresent "good heavens" was true. Maybe my words planted a seed, and I began to form my understanding of heaven on earth.

Maybe my onstage "good heavens" affirmation led to the inspiration to laminate the cats' health papers and gain the approval of the company manager. I'll never know. I do know I appreciated the inspiration, and the new-found respect my precise action brought me. I appreciated feeling like I finally belonged. Yet, these things were not the real gifts in this situation.

The deeper blessing is always a process of incarnation—*embodying* the truth of divine being. The deeper blessing is an ongoing practice of divinely aligned perception plus action. Again, it is trusting God *and* tethering our camel, too. Shifting our perception changes our experience; and experience changes our perception. We simultaneously think ourselves into a new way of living as we live ourselves into a new way of thinking.[9] Through a heart-full balance of thought and action, we embody a dazzling-yet-humble remembrance of the poised, present, infinite, intimate holiness, expressing through every detail of our lives. Our indestructible divine nature is indelibly laminated in place by God—and because this is so, we are free to celebrate the glories of good heavens on earth. We return home to a holy place we have never left.

Reflections

Head: Notice where you feel like you don't belong. Notice where you reject yourself.

Heart: Divine Love, reveal my dazzling-yet-humble self as one who always belongs exactly where I am, as I am.

Hands: Find a creative way to include someone who may feel excluded.

---

[9] Many people in my denomination say, "Change your thinking, change your life." Richard Rohr, author, priest, and founder of The Center for Action and Contemplation wrote, "We do not think ourselves into a new way of living. We live ourselves into a new way of thinking." In my text, I combined the two because I believe changed thinking and changed living work together.

INNOCENCE 4

"Every act of rebellion expresses a nostalgia for innocence and an appeal to the essence of being."
—Albert Camus

The tour continued and my confidence grew. The cast became our family, and we all shared the cats as pets. I kept them safe and healthy. Most of the time, Grandma did a good job onstage. Most of the time…

We were onstage in Seattle. Grandma was acting up a storm in her scene with Julie Harris. I waited behind the stage-left scenery for the cat hand-off. Suddenly, I heard a human screech and an alarming cat-snarl. I peered through a crack in the set and saw Grandma—A.K.A. The Anti-Christ—trying to disembowel Julie. The scene continued and Julie held on. When Julie arrived stage-left to give me the cat, Grandma's stiff claws were embedded in her neck. There was nothing to do but yank at Grandma and set them both free.

Julie went back onstage to finish her scene. I trotted to my dressing room holding a smirking Grandma. I passed her off to Hugh, grabbed a tube of Neosporin, and galloped back-stage-right for Julie's next exit. The stage manager looked up from calling cues and arched her left eyebrow at me.

"Oops," I said with a grimace.

Julie exited for a moment.

"Ouch," she said as I slapped a thin film of Neosporin on her pin-prick neck wounds. She went back onstage, and the show continued.

The whole cast knew Grandma scratched the star of the show. I gripped my tell-tale Neosporin tube and entered the walk of shame back to our dressing room. Once there, I stood in the doorway, and watched Hugh solemnly stare at the wayward Grandma, who sat on the white Formica counter in front of the illuminated make-up mirror. Grandma assumed a nonchalant attitude about what she had done. She stretched her haughty hind leg and groomed herself.

"What were you thinking?" Hugh said.

Grandma kept on licking.

"You know, your understudy could replace you at any time," Hugh added.

I knew he was invoking a vague *All About Eve*-like warning, reminding Grandma of a film in which another catty understudy usurps the star. Grandma glanced at Hugh with disdain then continued her grooming ritual.

That was near the end of the run. When the show closed, Grandma's original owner let us keep the now famous kitty. After the tour, Hugh, Grandma, Miranda, and I moved to Southern California. The cats endured a miserable ride in a rental truck across the country. Once we arrived in our new home, we pampered both kitties until they passed away years later. Several other company members have died as well. The company manager who loved my laminating and a fellow cast-member both died of AIDS. Julie Harris died in 2013.

They've all left the theater.

During the run of *Lettice and Lovage*, we left the theater

every night after the show through the stage door with the cats in their carriers. People waiting for autographs would often gasp and exclaim, "Oh, look, here are the cats!" They took little notice of Hugh and me, even though we were in the play, too. It is humbling to be upstaged by a cat.

Animals onstage are compelling because they are unpredictable. Grandma proved that. But there's also an attractive innocence to animals, a poised sense of "I deserve to be here, and I am enough just as I am." Animals inhabit the theater of innocence. They touch the essence of being. Even on the days when they mangle a celebrity, or perform below expectations, they simply look in the mirror, lick their hind leg, and move on.

Many humans walk upon the earth feeling guilty and undeserving. We believe we don't have the right to take up space on the stage called planet earth. Certainly, at the start of *Lettice and Lovage*, I felt this way about the literal stage. I felt like I didn't belong. I was certain I hadn't earned my spot in this prestigious tour. I felt inadequate and I worried because I didn't know about Shakespeare and such, like I suspected all the other actors did. Now I see it didn't matter, because Shakespeare knows me. He knows all of us.

Shakespeare knows "the world is a stage, and we are merely players."[10] He observes how we "strut and fret this hour upon the stage" called planet earth. He has heard our "tales of sound and fury, told by a foolish ego, our doubts and fears signifying nothing."[11]

Shakespeare understands the challenges of being human,

---

10 *As You Like It*, by William Shakespeare: "All the world's a stage, and all the men and women merely players."
11 *Macbeth*, by William Shakespeare: "Life's but a walking shadow, a poor player, that struts and frets his hour upon the stage, and then is heard no more. It is a tale told by an idiot, full of sound and fury, signifying nothing."

but also acknowledges the innate, amazing, grace-full innocence underlying all our human frailties. He reminds us to mine the sweetness in adversity, even the adversities we find in ourselves. When Grandma scratched Julie Harris in act two of *Lettice and Lovage* that dark day in Seattle, she wasn't bad—she was just having a moment.

Grandma and Miranda awakened me to a deeper knowing of our shared innocence. They were two poised yet imperfect performers. They were pure in heart, doing the best they could, excelling at being their sweet, catty, and sometimes scratchy selves. They were purring bundles of love, flailing demons, chaotic divas, and peaceful, sleepy souls. They could turn from darkness to light and back again in a moment. They were whole as God made them and completely worthy of love.

With Grandma and Miranda in mind, maybe we can extend some grace to ourselves when we spend time wallowing in chronic guilt and undeserving thoughts—when we erroneously believe we need to earn our place in heaven on earth. Maybe we can forgive ourselves when we wield our claws and hiss at life. Before we "shuffle off this mortal coil," before we leave the divine earthbound theater, maybe we can smile at our mindless clawing and anchor in innocence.[12] We can "do as the heavens have done and forget our 'evil,' for with this we forgive ourselves."[13] We can trust that our performance as humans-becoming is more than enough. We are beautiful just as we are. Just like Grandma and Miranda.

---

[12] *Hamlet,* by William Shakespeare: "To die, to sleep; To sleep, perchance to dream—For in that sleep of death what dreams may come, when we have shuffled off this mortal coil."

[13] *The Winter's Tale,* by William Shakespeare. "Do as the heavens have done, forget your evil; With them forgive yourself."

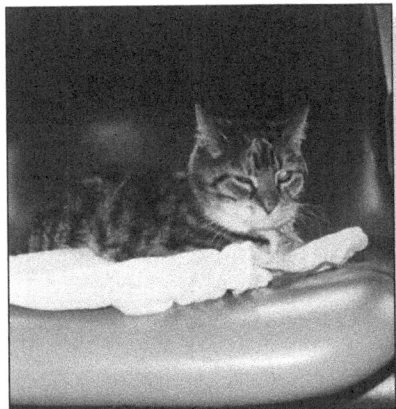 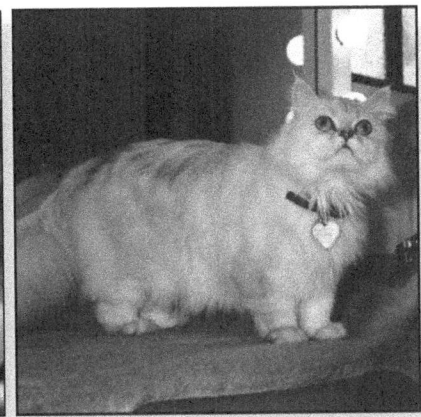

Grandma in the airport.   *Miranda in front of her make-up mirror.*

Reflections

Head: Where do you hold unresolved guilt?

Heart: Divine Love, help me honor my innate innocence.

Hands: Find your innocence by seeing innocence in others. Also look for opportunities to forgive, apologize, or make amends.

PART TWO:

SLAM-DANCING IN CHURCH

INTO THE CHRYSALIS

"We must not...assume that our schedule is our own to manage but allow it to be arranged by God."
—Dietrich Bonhoeffer

It was our second Sunday in Southern California. I only had two friends in my new town. They were both busy and Hugh was away with our single car. I was bored, so I went to church. The only church within walking distance was The North Hollywood Church of Religious Science. I strolled a few blocks and entered a white building with a tall steeple. The red pews were packed with a diverse, lively crowd. The message was about love and personal responsibility. When the minister said "We bless all paths to God" in his final prayer, I knew I had found a spiritual community.

I got more involved and learned the church was part of the Religious Science denomination, also known as the Science of Mind. The religion is based on the writings of Ernest Holmes, a scholar who was part of the new thought/ancient wisdom movement in America. This movement seeks the commonalities that connect all mystical paths. New thought/ancient wisdom teachings belong to the perennial wisdom tradition.

Perennial wisdom refers to universal spiritual truths that pop up in many faiths like perennial flowers. Perennial wisdom teaches that a divine reality exists as the source of everything. Some refer to this divine reality as God. Perennial teachers believe all of existence is one with God—but there's a catch. Ernest Holmes wrote, "We believe that the kingdom of heaven is within us. Yet we *experience* this kingdom to the degree that we become *conscious* of it."[ii]

We must become conscious of divinity to experience divinity. But rather than become conscious of divinity, we often succumb to an illusion of separation. We spend our lives either consciously or unconsciously seeking union with a source from which we have never left. We're like a puppy chasing its tail. We chase after something that already belongs to us.

In the Science of Mind—now called Centers for Spiritual Living—we teach that God is not a man in heaven, but a cosmic force, the source and substance of all things seen and unseen. God is love. We believe God creates matter out of itself so the whole cosmos is love. Humanity is one with God; God interconnects all things. The cosmos is the body of God, the body of love.

The ultimate purpose of existence is to remember who we are and express oneness through love. We have been endowed with a creative power which we can use to *be* the way of love or *be in* the way of love. Our creative power expresses through belief. The quality of our belief affects the quality of our lives. So for example, as we focus on lack, we experience lack. As we focus on love, we experience love.

I participated in classes in this teaching and became a practitioner. A practitioner serves a spiritual community by offering prayer, spiritual guidance, and general assistance. As I served, my interest in spirituality grew. I was still singing part-time, working for an opera company, and doing side gigs as a soloist or chorister. I also worked as a nurse in an outpatient psychiatric program.

Then I became restless. I liked singing, but began to resent getting callbacks for auditions. Most singers crave callbacks. For me, it felt like too much work to put on a dress, panty hose, and pointy high heels to go sing my best 16-bars in a stark studio in front of some casting director who could give a crap. My restlessness grew until I realized it was time to stop singing professionally. I decided to put myself through ministerial school and took a job as a corporate trainer in a medical device company to support this plan.

I told Hugh about my plans for a new career path on Valentine's Day when we were sitting at a table for two looking at the menu at Jerry's Deli in Sherman Oaks.

"I need to tell you something," I said as I switched my gaze to the red-checked tablecloth.

Hugh looked up from the menu. I hesitated to tell him about this new direction and expected a long discussion about it. When Hugh married me, I was a singer. I wasn't sure how he'd feel about my ministerial aspirations, even though he has an active spiritual life himself.

"I want to quit singing and become a minister," I said.

"Great," he replied with encouragement in his voice. Then he looked at the menu again to make his choice. "I think I'll have the chicken fettuccine."

That was it. This was the first of many conversations with him when my fear of disrupting our shared life was met with unquestioning support. There was no third degree. He didn't second guess my intentions or share concerns about the impact of my changes on his life. He just expressed trust in my new adventure. Hugh's trust helped me trust myself.

So often the process of making a major change brings fear and hesitation—fear of dissolving old patterns and hesitation to surrender to the unknown. But omnipresent heaven exists in uncertainty, too—for uncertainty can be a catalyst for metamorphosis.

Does a caterpillar trust going into a chrysalis to dissolve into mush will give him wings? I wouldn't trust that for a minute. The plan seems completely unreliable. But we're all here to grow wings in one way or another. We're all here to learn to trust. Learning to trust connects us with our true nature. Learning to trust helps us fly.

Reflections

Head: What new path seeks to emerge through you? Do you trust your new aspirations?

Heart: Divine Love, help me to enter the chrysalis before I know the possibility of wings.

Hands: Spend a day acting as if your heart's desire is already accomplished.

DANCES WITH DOGS | 45

Life in California - Buster the Bunny, Bonnie, Miranda, Santa Claus, Audrey, Hugh, and Guinea Pig Bob.

PUPPY-MAGEDDON

"Be willing to be used by God; be willing to be used by Truth. Be willing to be an instrument through which Truth reveals Itself."

—Joel Goldsmith

After Grandma and Miranda passed away, our friends, Debbie and Jeff, suggested we get a dog. Debbie and Jeff had a Vizsla, and their dog's mother was pregnant again with a single puppy.

"If you adopt our dog's sister, we'll be family," Debbie told me.

I met Debbie and Jeff when I went to Duke for my degree in nursing. They were two of my best friends and through a series of synchronicities, we all ended up in Southern California. I liked the idea of becoming family—but we didn't want a dog. I'd just finished ministerial school and was serving part-time at the church in North Hollywood, while also managing my day job as a medical corporate trainer. *A dog will be too much work, too time consuming,* I thought.

Just to make sure we didn't want a dog, I did some research about Vizslas on the internet. According to Google, Vizslas are horrible high-maintenance animals. They are hunter-pointers, bred to be sporting dogs that need to run at least four miles every day. The internet stated they are affectionate and needy, and prone to cling to their human companions like 50-pound Velcro appendages. Vizslas were bred to be bed-warmers for hunters. This means they must sleep pinned to their humans, under the covers. A Vizsla will dig a hole to China in your blankets until you lift up the bedding and let them under.

The internet warned the breed was an enormous pain in the butt. Still, the Vizslas online were awfully cute, with their long floppy ears and sleek russet coats. So we decided to visit the newborn puppy in question. When we met her, smelled her puppy breath, stroked her silky ears, and snuggled her warm body close to our hearts, she seduced us. We decided to invest in this little maniac. We named her Stella, brought her home, and once again ruined our lives for the love of an animal.

Baby Stella's first day home.

On Stella's first day home, she peed on our couch, chased our bunny, and embarked on a chewing crusade. We spent several thousand dollars on dog training so she could learn the basics of obedience, such as sit, stay, and heel. Like many of us, she learned obedience, but only followed the rules when it was convenient. Despite her costly training, Stella continued to shred shoes, blankets, plants, and furniture. She ate a head-sized hole in the arm of our custom-made chaise lounge.

One morning about six months into puppy-mageddon, I went to the post office to mail my Christmas cards. I left Stella uncrated for 20 minutes. I came back home to discover while I was away, our pup pawed open a bathroom cabinet and excavated a new Costco-sized box of feminine hygiene products. She ravaged the box and tore up a gross of tampons. A blizzard of tiny white carcasses glared at me from the dark blue bathroom tiles. It was a canine crime scene.

Stella's mournful eyes and hunched posture indicated she would suffer the consequences of dining on the gross. A few hours later, she vomited several pints of yellow slime on our cream-colored sofa, so I took her to the vet.

Disgraced, I slumped in the vet's waiting room.

"Did you have to eat tampons?" I said to Stella, through gritted teeth. "Couldn't it have been a flip-flop, or a squeaky toy, or something less embarrassing?"

I was appalled at my lack of dog parenting skills. But the kind vet techs ushered me through my shame with other naughty dog stories. One tech knew a Beagle who ate a leotard. Another treated a Pug who ingested a box of uncooked elbow macaroni then inflated like a beach ball when he drank water. They assured me Stella would be okay.

Stella stayed in the animal hospital overnight for observation. The tampons frolicked through her intestinal tract and exited out her hind end. We took her back home with gratitude for the happy outcome—and one other major consequence.

Heaven on earth reveals itself in adversity. It was probably a combination of guilt, regret, and love—but after the great tampon caper, I became completely obsessed with Stella's well-being. I vowed to devote my life to her care.

I'll teach her to channel her tampon-eating fervor into something constructive, I told myself. That meant exercise. We hiked five miles every morning and went to the dog park in the afternoons. On weekends, we drove to the beach in Ventura, California, to let her run off-leash. Her best-possible-life was my purpose and everything we did together made me love her more.

One Sunday, late afternoon, Stella and I went to the beach as the sun set over the Pacific Ocean. Seagulls screeched in the distance while the waves hustled to the shore. I threw a neon yellow tennis ball into the waves. Stella bounded in after it and brought it back to me, hundreds of times. I wore an extra-large purple T-shirt with a graphic depicting our animal ministry at the North Hollywood Church. A tall blonde, middle-aged woman with a golden retriever approached me.

"So there's an animal ministry at your church?"

"Yes, there is," I replied.

"What kind of a church is it?"

"Interfaith. Metaphysical. We bless all paths to God. A lot of us really like animals, too."

"Oh, sometimes I go to a church like that in Ventura," she said.

We discovered our churches were the same denomination, and we chatted for a few minutes. Stella punctuated the conversation by yelping at the tennis ball in my hand, insisting I throw it for her. The woman with the golden retriever said goodbye and walked away.

"You know what?" I said to Stella as the woman disappeared beyond a jetty. "If that church in Ventura ever has a job opening, I'll check it out. For you."

Two weeks later, the minister at the Ventura church resigned. I felt a little sick to my stomach. I got a Master of Divinity degree so I could be a hospital chaplain someday, maybe, but I didn't want to be a church minister. I didn't pay attention to my ministerial school classes about how to run a church. I was not equipped for this job.

But some higher heaven seemed to call me. I couldn't ignore the timing, so with zombie-like dedication, I auto-piloted through the steps of applying. I submitted a resume and an unconventional photo—a headshot of Stella and me. The search committee liked that I had a dog in my picture. They asked me to come up for a weekend to undergo several interviews, give a sermon, and teach a workshop.

I did not pray to get this job. I didn't beg God or try to cajole reality to do my bidding like I did with the Broadway tour. On the drive home from my weekend interview at the church, I called the competition—my best friend, Marc—who was also vying for the position.

"Dude, you can have it," I told him. "It's not a good fit for me."

Several months after my application, the church made me an offer. I still wasn't sure I would be a good minister—in fact, I was pretty sure I didn't even *want* to be a minister—but I said yes.

I think back to that exchange on the beach with an unknown woman, a golden retriever, and Stella barking at a tennis ball. It seemed like a meaningless encounter, a speed-date where we discussed spirituality and church for five minutes. Did that trivial moment shift my consciousness and alter the course of my life? Chances are, I wouldn't have noticed or considered the opening in the Ventura church had I not crashed into such synchronicity.

Maybe synchronicity, like coincidence, is heaven's way of remaining anonymous. Stella called me to devotion. Even though it started with devotion to a dog, the divine knew devotion to anything can be devotion to everything. Devotion sent a p-mail (prayer-mail) that said: "Use Bonnie for your higher purpose. She will be an instrument through which greater love can reveal itself." Heaven answered the p-mail and used my pointer-dog to point me to a church.

Heaven on earth saw an opportunity. It found a tiny fissure in my guarded heart. There it planted a seed. The seed ignored my reluctance and catapulted me into ministry—a ministry that would eventually teach me to love beyond my willingness to love.

Reflections

Head: What is the focus of your devotion? Does your devotion want to grow?

Heart: Divine Love, help me discover unlimited outlets for my devotion.

Hands: Expand your devotion. Do something you've always wanted to do with great love; or do something that feels challenging and see what happens when you ask love to assist. Love beyond your willingness to love.

BEFRIENDING FAILURE

"Every adversity, every failure, every heartache carries with it the seed of an equal or greater benefit."
—Napoleon Hill

I never saw the woman from the beach again. For many years, I didn't know if she was an angel or the devil. Because in the beginning, my church gig felt awful.

Just in case anyone from my early or current church reads this, I should say that *everything you're about to read was all my fault*. In the early days of ministry, I saw life through a lens of unexamined shame. I was in mental/emotional hell, and I didn't know it. Eventually I grew into compassion for myself and others. Eventually I learned to befriend what looked like rejection or failure. Eventually I moved into immense appreciation for what happened not *to* me, but *for* me in those early years of hapless ministry. But it took a while.

The congregation I inherited was sweet and well-meaning. Many of them were attached to the former minister and saw me only as a pallid replacement. Others wanted me to be happy and wanted to like me. They made valiant efforts to be kind and welcoming. Yet, I was completely unprepared. I was unprepared for the complexities of running a church in a small town, and there were many. I did not know that every time I stood in a checkout line to purchase something personal—say a 12-pack of pastel granny panties—I would encounter a congregant. And all panties aside, I did not know full-time ministry would reveal a gaggle of my unaddressed frailties.

Despite my background in performing, I am an introvert. In church, there was no script or music to hide behind. It was just me on a stage with a microphone and my innermost thoughts. Every Sunday when I offered my sermon, my hands trembled, and my voice shook. I galloped through deep spiritual teachings, speaking way too quickly, just so I could slink off the terrifying stage away from the judgment of others.

The gay men liked me because they often do. Some of the lesbians thought I was too straight. Some of the straight people thought I was too gay. The conservatives thought I was too liberal, and the liberals thought I was too conservative. The ex-military rallied because I forgot to applaud them on Veteran's Day. A few months in, I quoted the Saint Francis prayer: "Lord, make me an instrument of Thy peace." A male feminist stomped out of the service because "Lord" implies "God is a man."

Some people thought I was too Christian. It's an interfaith church, but there are a lot of former Christians in the congregation wounded by early church experiences. I'm no hellfire and brimstone preacher, but I love the gentle paradoxes of Jesus. I had a rose quartz rosary that I stashed in my cleavage so my new congregation wouldn't see.

"Be patient. Stay tucked in there until they trust me," I told Jesus. Thankfully, Jesus cooperated.

Others criticized my clothes. One day, I received an anonymous envelope. I opened it, glanced down, and saw a patch of skin in a magazine photo. I pulled out the pages gingerly, thinking the envelope might contain a perverted collage of penises and whatnot. Side note: my mind is often in the gutter, but to be fair, I used to encounter exhibitionists on a semi-regular basis. I know we're not supposed to make light of such things, and I have great compassion for women who suffer trauma from this type of criminal behavior. But I was a magnet—probably because of my nursing career.

Fresh out of nursing school, I spent a year serving patients with spinal cord injuries. My work involved repeated urinary catheterizations on multiple men. To be blunt, I stuck tubes in penises, one after the other, like an assembly line, eight hours a night. I saw a lot of the little fellow in the hospital and therefore was unperturbed when I encountered a plethora of exposed wieners on the subways of New York, in Macy's, on a golf course, or at Coney Island on the Tilt-a-Whirl. Someone would reveal themselves, and I'd roll my eyes and say, "Sir: please put Mr. Tiny away and show me something I haven't seen a thousand times."

Still, I didn't want that experience in church. To my relief, the skin-photos I received in my letter were not a genitalia collage, just pictures of fully clothed women in business wear. A handwritten, unsigned note scrawled, "Try dressing more like this, Reverend Bonnie!"

Another congregant, an elderly woman, said I didn't have a big enough rotation of clothes. (I am happiest in black pants and a colorful top). "Men can get away with wearing the same suit every week," she scolded, "but women need to change their outfits more often than you do." Then she added, "I'll get you a gift certificate to my favorite dress shop!"

"Is church really about my clothes?" I asked politely. I really wanted to know. But the congregant was insulted, and I never heard from her again.

A few months later, a man cornered me in the church kitchen with an arsenal of complaints.

"Your sermons are boring, and you speak in platitudes. But the *worst* thing about you, Reverend Bonnie, is this: you apologize too much."

"I'm sorry," I said.

The new church didn't like my theology. My faith evolved during my tour of ministerial school. I was losing interest in my prior Broadway-show-manifestation-spirituality phase and was beginning to wonder if maybe we were treating God like an ATM. I questioned our tendency to push magic prayer buttons to get God to spit out cash and other accoutrements according to our material needs. *Is "better stuff" the source of our happiness?* I thought. *Isn't there a higher will at play in our lives, perhaps a divine essence with insight beyond our personal agendas?* I noticed my own tendency to pummel God with prayers to get what I wanted and began to seek mystery over mastery.

I was timid about speaking to the congregation about such things—a lot of people in our denomination at the time wanted concrete strategies to "fix" their lives. Tentatively, I offered gentle messages that celebrated our astounding inability to describe the infinite. I shared my delight in human frailty shaken and stirred by life's challenges. I expressed the joys and sorrows of impermanence. I brazenly cultivated a preference for unanswerable questions over quick fix-it answers. The congregation was unhappy with my mystical brand of metaphysics. They also disdained my playful irreverence.

One Sunday I spoke about a divine revelation. Sadly, I don't remember what the revelation was, but I do remember wanting to downplay it. So many spiritual teachers are filled with hubris around their own "specialness." I didn't want to appear special because I'm not. I told the congregation, "Spiritual revelations usually happen when you're not looking for them. I recently had a revelation in the middle of the night. I woke out of a deep sleep, staggered to the bathroom, and heard the voice of God!"

I acted it out. I plowed across the stage, miming tripping over dog toys, and pulling an imaginary nightie out of my butt-crack.

The butt-crack hit the fan. People were mortified by my humanity, and I was bewildered. Because it was a great acting choice, and it was funny. Seriously funny. *Maybe ministers aren't supposed to have butt cracks,* I wondered. *Do they think I'm a Ken doll down there?*[14]

The church began to shrink. The membership roster vomited congregants onto Laurel Street where they scuttled to Unity or the Unitarians, the churches with better-equipped ministers, the ministers who didn't pantomime pulling sleepwear out of their fannies. The money scampered off with the departing members and filled the coffers of the other more dignified churches. I felt like the eleventh plague of Egypt, swallowed by the shame of rejection.

What made it worse was despite my interest in human frailty and mystery, I felt I had to *prove* I was capable. I was raised to be an achiever, so I schemed to give the illusion of success and confidence. My lesser instincts told me to measure success in terms of worldly attributes, such as attendance and money. When I didn't "manifest" those things immediately, I denied my desperation and pretended I was fine. At the time, I couldn't see the power of acknowledging my sacred vulnerability.

Back then, I called my church *The Church of the Corn*. It refers to a Stephen King book, *The Children of the Corn*. The children of

---

14 One of my proofreaders asked why I chose to compare myself to Ken vs. Barbie. In *Barbie and Ruth, the Story of the World's Most Famous Doll and the Woman Who Created Her,* author Robin Gerber writes of many meetings at Mattel Inc. to address the nature of Ken's bottom. They needed to make it smooth and not sexy. As I recall, Barbie's bottom is shapelier –hence my comparison to Ken.

the corn hate strangers. They emerge like shadows and stare at newcomers with dead eyes conveying, "Go away, you are not one of us."

That was the relationship I *perceived* with many in my congregation. A good chunk of them judged me and wanted me to change—or leave. I wanted to leave. I felt I would never be enough for them. Yet I couldn't sacrifice my odd blend of deep mysticism and playful irreverence just to please people. I had an inkling that staying true to my whimsy was essential to God's plan. So how could I stay and remain authentic? How could I be authentic and avoid failure? How could someone like me possibly survive and eventually celebrate ministry in *The Church of the Corn*?

Again, a presence greater than my small self offered me a new view. I could stay, remain authentic, and change my relationship with failure. I could *befriend* failure.

The notion of befriending failure did not appeal to me. "Thanks a lot, God," I said. But soon the challenge tugged at the leg of my redundant black pants, like an impatient child. The urgency of this new idea grew, so I contemplated: *Is it possible that failure isn't failure? Maybe failure isn't a monster teacher but a master teacher. Maybe failure is a paradox of success in disguise—because examined failure carries the seeds of the better yet to be.*

Paradox points to spiritual truth. The conscious embrace of failure expands the heart into wholeness. When we see beyond the illusion of opposites such as success and failure, we discover the true self abiding as an unfathomable allness that contains everything as one. The true self rests as spaciousness and peace. It regards failure as an aspect of success—an aspect that has no power unless we invest it with meaning. And focusing on the true self in the face of perceived failure moves us from victim to unconditional victor.

I was nowhere near this state of awareness early in my

ministry. I didn't know if I *could* befriend failure. But I bravely pulled my nightie out of my non-butt crack and kept moving forward to see what love would do.

Reflections

Head: What is your relationship with failure? What do you tell yourself about failure? Is your story about failure spiritually true?

Heart: Divine Love, help me live as the true self that rests beyond opposites.

Hands: Consider an alleged failure and find 10 hidden gifts in it. Offer this practice to someone else who struggles with a perception of failure.

THE NAKED BURRITO

"The mind is its own place, and in itself can make a heaven of hell, a hell of heaven."

— John Milton

Hard-core metaphysical teachers might ask, "What was in your consciousness to create that challenging church scenario?" "How did you manifest *The Church of the Corn*?" "Why did you create such an epic experience of failure?"

Sometimes bad or uncomfortable things happen. People will be unintentionally or intentionally unkind. They will send you pictures in envelopes of church-appropriate clothes that some might mistake for an envelope of penis pictures. It happens. People will tell you to stop apologizing. They will reject your authentic self.

We can't let the personal ego play God and pretend it's *all* about us while we deny the responsibility of others. At the same time, victory through failure is achieved when we dispassionately observe the ways we punch ourselves with what happens. A good life is not about what happens to us. A good life grows when we become conscious about *what we do with what happens*.

Our brains process information non-stop to make meaning out of life's events. Meaning arises from our state of mind. If we live in a persistent inner climate of shameful distress, when something unwanted happens, we weaponize it. We say, "This *proves* there is something wrong with me." We self-flagellate with blame, despair, and regret. Self-flagellation is a form of resistance that gives unnecessary power to an undesired situation. The undesired power grows in strength as we repeat our meanings. The thoughts we repeat most are the thoughts we wish we didn't have. Repeated meanings dig neural grooves—or neural graves—in our brains. "A groove is a grave with the ends kicked out."[15]

During the early years at *The Church of the Corn*, I formed a lot of neural graves. Then an experience in a restaurant awakened me to the power of making meaning and how we use it against ourselves. On this particular day, a cashier offered me a stunning example of what the mind can do with mere words.

A woman named Becky was our board president in the early years of my ministry. Becky was one of the reasons I was able to stay when my position was difficult. She believed in me and worked tirelessly to co-create the eventual well-being of our church.

Becky and I often had lunch together after Sunday service, usually at a Mexican fast-food restaurant. The food was nourishing and tasty, but we also liked the cashier. He was a striking, athletic, 30-ish man who was gracious to the customers. He had a sparkling Zorro-like smile and wore a tight black polo shirt over his rippled pectorals.

I suppose I had an old lady crush on him. It may have been wrong to objectify this young man, but I truly did not intend to use him in an impure manner. I'm old. I'm a married, menopausal minister, for God's sake. The young man riveted my attention because he reminded me of the boys in high school—the popular

---

[15] This quote refers to "A rut is a grave with the end kicked out." Attributed to Vince Havner, Earl Nightengale, and others.

ones who were in-crowd and unattainable. All I wanted was to charm him when I ordered my food. To make him like me. To be young again.

One day, Becky and I went to the restaurant after a difficult morning at the church. I had preached a tepidly received sermon. I could tell the congregation was disappointed, and I wondered if I would ever be who they wanted me to be. Becky opened the restaurant door for me and I shuffled in with my head down. It was a late lunch, I was hungry, and I hoped to eat away my pain. I wanted a huge meal to fill the void of despair that scraped at my soul. I stood in the line to order and looked at the overhead menu. I saw an item called The Naked Burrito—a vegetarian burrito wrapped in a whole wheat tortilla, minus excessive trimmings such as cheese, sour cream, and salsa. That's what I wanted.

As I waited in the food line beside Becky, I admired the handsome cashier's physique—then felt a twinge of angst.

"Becky," I whispered. "I'm starving and I want The Naked Burrito. Do you know how big it is?"

"Nope, never had it," she replied. "Ask the hot cashier."

"You ask him."

"I don't want a naked burrito." Becky said. "I'm gay."

"Lucky for you," I answered. "But seriously, how am I gonna ask him, 'How big is your naked burrito?'"

"Try making eye contact," Becky replied.

"I'm scared I'll look at his pants."

"Ask him to show you a picture of it," Becky said.

"You're not helping."

We stopped our whispered girl fight and retreated into a contemplative silence as we waited our turn to order. The situation was fraught with hazards akin to my teenage years. There was nowhere to look, I was afraid of saying the wrong thing, and I felt the potential for unexplainable blushing.

We got to the front of the line. Becky ordered her food, and again, refused to size-up my burrito request. So when it was my turn, I paused as the cashier waited expectantly. I gazed at the ceiling as if I was still pondering my dietary needs, and I found the answer in the graying fiberglass tiles. *"Order something else—anything else,"* went through my mind. *"Just spare yourself the agony of inquiring about the size of the man's naked burrito."*

"Um...can I please have the Mexican quinoa salad?" I asked, ditching my original plan.

My order complete, I slunk to a booth where Becky and I marveled at the still small 17-year-old girl that manages to rear up in old ladies.

Later, I wondered, *Why can't a grown woman in a Mexican restaurant ask for what she wants? Why couldn't I just say the words?*

I have literally walked on hot coals for personal growth. I have karate-chopped boards with my bare hands in spiritual workshops. I have sung opera with an orchestra, managed complex medical emergencies, and was currently slogging my way through running a church. What is so hard about asking an attractive man to reveal the size of his naked burrito? How did this cashier render me speechless?

It wasn't the cashier's fault. It was my fertile mind.

Obviously, there's sexual innuendo at play in this tale. I've always been an expert at innuendo because of nursing and singing. Nurses get comfortable with body parts. We stick tubes, fingers, and other implements into every orifice. The more we keep it casual and fun, the easier it is for the patient. This lends itself to a cheerful disregard for the humiliations of being human.

Learning to sing is a surprisingly physical endeavor that evokes a similar nonchalance about the body. Plus, there's epic lust in opera. The fervor of the music added to the steamy nature of many opera plots inspires good-natured backstage banter.

In the case of the naked burrito, a randy inner monologue stepped center stage to paralyze my tongue. It's one thing to trip over your naked burrito in a restaurant. The bigger message of this story speaks to the power we give to words in all circumstances.

When I worked on the Broadway tour, my thoughts—the words I spoke to myself—got in the way. I was insecure about my right to be there and wondered if I would be rejected. It made the job more challenging than it needed to be at first, but ultimately, I triumphed and conquered my insecurities. I started speaking spiritual truth to myself, but it only went so far. Ministry in a challenging church gave me a way to grow deeper.

We are infinite beings, and our healing never stops. Those on a spiritual path enjoy the fruits of a never-ending obstacle course to inspire us and help us grow. Yes, the call to become a full-time minister was a call to greater devotion—but also a call to a healing upgrade. Church was a place where my insecurities could ratchet up several hundred notches, a place where I could feel more flawed than ever before.

My early ministry inner monologue was something like this: *What was I thinking? I'm terrible at this. People don't like me. I'm too ordinary. I'm too weird. I don't fit in. I feel like a loser. I'm failing. I'm ashamed...*

Mere words, but I believed them. I made meaning. I invested power in these words through repetition, and my investment caused more neural graves, plus more meaning making. Everything around me looked like evidence to support my "head-lines."

We create headlines to tell a story about circumstances. In an instant, we can turn an innocent naked burrito into an embarrassment. We can turn an uncomfortable, changing church into proof of our unworthiness. We turn heaven into hell. Then we gather visible "evidence" to support the meanings we have made. Because we do not believe what we see. We *see* what we *believe*.

Our news stories become reality to us, and this self-imposed reality limits our capacity to choose from the infinite menu of life.

The naked burrito incident was a blessing because it was ridiculous enough to get my attention. We will always make meaning out of what happens, but we don't have to let our meanings make us. Life can't define us when we define life. From this new point of insight, I contemplated, *"What do I really want from life's menu? What do I want from the menu called ministry? How do I let go of old head-lines to bring forth magnificence?"*

Reflections

Head: What "neural graves" are you forming? In other words, what life-negating "head-lines" do you tell yourself?

Heart: Divine Love, help me find truthful, life-affirming meanings in all circumstances.

Hands: As you go about your day, affirm good in everything. Say thank you for small blessings; look for goodness in life's challenges. When you can't find goodness, ask Divine Love to help you see anew.

THE MIRROR 9

"You are here to work on yourself. Only yourself. Thank anyone who gives you the opportunity."
—George I. Gurdjieff

I contacted a well-known psychic to gain advice on how to do better with my church. We had a phone appointment, and the first thing she said was, "You have to stop rolling your eyes."

"I do *not* roll my eyes," I replied as I rolled my eyes.

"You're doing it now, aren't you?"

I confessed. The psychic told me even when people can't see your eyes rolling back in your head, they can feel it.

"Eye rolling emits a certain disdainful energy," she said.

She was right. I was an eye roller. So I thought about a George Gurdjieff quote: "You are here to work on yourself, only yourself. Thank anyone who gives you the opportunity." I decided to work on myself, and I thanked my church for the opportunity.

Rumi wrote, in God's voice speaking to humanity: "You have no idea how hard I've looked for a gift to bring you. Nothing seemed right. What's the point of bringing gold to the gold mine, or water to the ocean? Everything I came up with was like taking spices to the Orient. It's no good giving my heart and my soul because you already have these. So I've brought you a mirror. Look at yourself and remember me."

God offers us a mirror. That mirror is existence—where outer life reflects inner being. If we don't like outer conditions, we can sometimes change what is happening as easily as changing lanes on the freeway. When we can't change lanes, we can look within and change our thoughts, meanings, and perceptions. The serenity prayer asks God to "grant me the serenity to accept the things I cannot change; the courage to change the things I can; and the wisdom to know the difference."

I would add a postscript to that prayer: "God always grants us the capacity to change ourselves." Often when we change inside, our outer conditions change. So when *The Church of the Corn* wouldn't change according to *my* plans, it became my mirror.

I looked at my "failings" in the mirror. I whined, then I prayed. At first my prayers were shallow, a flurry of unskillful fixer-uppers. I wanted to "get over it, get on with it, and get it right." I prayed according to my level of insecurity and impatience. I had little trust in a power greater than my ego and even less trust in God's divine timing.

Again, I went against my own mystical leanings, and treated God like an ATM, hoping the ultimate power of the cosmos would spit out results according to my schedule.

"I am a successful minister with an immense church," I affirmed. "Everyone likes me." "Money flows into our bank account." I slapped at the infinite with a spiritual sledgehammer.

My plan was to manifest outer props that would "fix" my shaky self-worth. Thankfully, my ATM prayers were ineffective and exhausting.

I had it backwards. We don't pray to rearrange our outer scenery. Instead, we pray to change ourselves, to align ourselves with greatness of heart. We look in the mirror to see the limits of our hard-edged egos' plans. We let go of our attachment to "proving" ourselves through outer manifestations. We see that a compassionate call to inner well-being abides beneath our frenzied attempts to "get it right." We align with this deeper sense of compassion and embrace love's design. Then we prepare for inner change with small prayers and micro-surrenders—one step at a time.

Through tiny prayers and trivial steps, I discovered *The Church of the Corn* was *The Church of the Corn* because I was *The Minister of the Corn*. The perceived rejection from my new church and my reactivity around it was a mirror of my self-rejection. My eye-rolling that expressed covert disdain was self-disdain in disguise. There were many internalized children of the corn stalking my egoic brain telling me: *You are not worthy. All the other ministers are better than you. You're doing it wrong, and no minister in her right mind takes a church job to please her dog.* The church kindly mirrored the grip these thoughts had on me.

Once I saw my inner monologue, I could address it. I could stop covering my self-judgment by projecting blame onto others. Then I could work on loving myself. This was a gift, and it took a while to unwrap it. Fortunately, love stepped in again and helped take the gift out of the bag.

When Hugh and I lived in the San Fernando Valley, we had a neighbor who was raised Catholic. One day I had a conversation with him, literally over his white picket fence. He talked about going to high school dances in the church social hall when he was a teenager. Every time his hormones got the best of him, and he snuggled too close to his partner on the dance floor, a nun struck out of nowhere, like a viper. Sister Mary Catherine. She wrenched the two dancers apart while exclaiming, with an Irish brogue, "Leave enough room for the Holy Spirit, young man!"

The prayers our egos generate—often desperate and controlling—leave little room for the Holy Spirit. The Holy Spirit does its finest work through our willingness to let go.

There was a distinct moment in my church where I let go—a turning point inspired by the failure to make someone happy. Somebody lodged a complaint about me. I don't remember the exact details, but I remember my reaction. Rather than acting all faux-mature and holy, I surrendered. I took the metaphorical hymnal out of my non-butt crack and asked for help. I didn't indulge my delusion about what a "real" minister should feel. Instead, I was honest about my pain. I emailed our practitioner prayer team and wrote: "Please pray for me. Give me the grace to deal with the inconsolable whiners in my life."

It was a little judgey and not particularly understanding of the pain of the complainer. But something shifted in that moment. The practitioners, at least some of them, thought my prayer request was funny. One said he laughed about it all day and every chuckle was a prayer on my behalf. Another emailed back and asked if my inconsolable whiners could meet-up with her inconsolable whiners. She envisioned a world where inconsolable whiners could whine together.

Somehow the practitioners' collective wit and wisdom allowed me to look in the mirror and see the face of the first inconsolable whiner I could address. That was me, *The Minister of the Corn*. I could start with compassion for myself, for the whiners, and for my whining about the whiners. Then, while the practitioners laughed at my humanity, I could laugh, too. As it often does, our shared laughter left some room for the Holy Spirit. Still a work in progress, I began a slow crawl toward an unknown, but undoubtedly better experience of the whole of spirit.

Reflections

Head: What does the outer mirror of your life tell you about the nature of your thoughts?

Heart: Divine Love, help me to leave some room for the whole of spirit.

Hands: Try something new. If you project disdain on others, project love. If you project fear on the world, think about faith. Notice how this practice changes you. Does your world change when you change?

UNQUALIFIED

"Let there be peace on earth and let it begin with me."
—Jill Jackson-Miller and Sy Miller

I've asked many spiritual teachers, "What's your biggest regret in leadership?" Usually they say, "The times I was unkind or impatient with someone."

Me too. I feel I *should* be kind to everyone, but I struggle with critics. I can't always find the grace to recognize the person criticizing me as love in a distressing disguise.

It's a tradition in our denomination to sing *The Peace Song* at the end of our church services. "Let there be peace on earth, and let it begin with me." It's a lovely song with a lovely message and people are attached to it. The song is difficult to sing. Very range-y, kind of like *The Star Spangled Banner*. There's a high note at the end. Most people don't want to sing the high note, and the people who do want to sing it probably shouldn't. Plus, when people sing *The Peace Song*, they hold hands and sway like the Who Chorus in *The Grinch Who Stole Christmas*. One day early in my ministry, my inner professional singer/actor got the best of me. I abandoned Whoville and took the song out of the service with little regard for peoples' devotion to it.

One particularly irate woman came into my office after

service to yell at me for my primitive action. I pushed back. I defended my desire to try something new and to help people loosen attachments. In the spirit of reinvention, I asked her to keep an open mind. I may have pointed out the irony of her rage about the removal of *The Peace Song*.

The hailstorm of criticism soon turned into a rampage about all my faults as a human being. The conversation dragged on way too long. True to my old patterns, at one point, I rolled my eyes. While rolling my eyes, I looked up at my bookshelf and saw a prayer stick I made during a class. It was a culturally appropriated Native American implement, a piece of driftwood with shells, ribbons, feathers, and beads attached. There was a piece of pink construction paper wrapped around the stick, with a prayer written on it, for a happy, healthy church. I was supposed to hold the stick while I prayed to help me focus, to allow the spirit of the prayer to assume form.

When I saw this item on my bookshelf during our heated conversation, it did not inspire prayer. Instead, it inspired the shower scene from *Psycho*. Just for a moment, I heard the screech of violins as I visualized myself using my prayer stick to pretend-stab in the vicinity of the angry congregant. I'm not proud of it, but that's what went through my mind.

The conversation ended without resolution. The enraged church member left feeling unheard, and I felt ashamed. I sat dejected in my office, wondering, *What is wrong with me? Why didn't I have the skills to fix this? What kind of a minster visualizes the Psycho shower scene?*

I looked at my office wall and saw my pictures of Lord Krishna, and the Buddha, and the Virgin of Guadalupe. I sighed and spoke out loud to them, "Do you think Billy-Freaking-Graham ever fantasized about bludgeoning a congregant?"

My spiritual heroes stared at me in silence, and I saw

accusation in their eyes. Clearly, I did not deserve to be in the same room with them. I was guilty of impersonating a minister.

I don't know what changed—maybe it was Krishna, or the Buddha, or the Blessed Virgin, or maybe grace —but suddenly something informed me that I was called to be a spiritual leader not because I am perfect. I was called because I am flawed. My flaws qualify me. I am qualified because I am unqualified.

If I am supposed to help people—to comfort them as they face their frailties, to inspire them to rise above their struggles into greatness—I am qualified to do so only if I have experienced and transcended struggles of my own. In that shameful moment, when I looked at my lack of qualifications, God's plan revealed itself to me in my heroic imperfections.

All of us humans are here to dwell in the paradoxes of woes and wonders. Unconditional love is meaningful only when there are conditions to overcome. Our imperfections, when held in absolute truth, provide a pathway for love beyond logic. Discovering the perfection of my imperfections was a paradox that opened me up to a gentler way of being in the world.

These days, I don't get quite as much criticism as before, probably because I love myself a little more and am better equipped to respond. Of course it helps to listen—to acknowledge when I've been careless with someone's feelings, to express empathy, and to see the person before me as love in distress.

What helps more though is to let peace begin with me. To let the healing begin with me. If I bring peace to my shortcomings, then the criticism of others can't derail me. When I accept my flaws as part of who I am, there is nothing to defend. Everything that was once "wrong" with me becomes part of what is "right" with me. From a perspective of greater self-compassion, inner peace creates outer peace. Then there is a chance I can "bless those who curse me" (Matthew 5:44). For when I see God in human strengths and frailties alike, I see how all critics—both inner and outer—are simply struggling to protect something within them that is perfectly imperfect.

Reflections

Head: Think of a time you felt unqualified. What gifts might be hidden in your perceived imperfection?

Heart: Divine Love, help me befriend my imperfections as perfect teachers.

Hands: Live life as an advanced game of befriending everything. "Bless those who curse you." Notice where it's easy, notice where it's difficult.

CHASING THE SHADOW

"Shame is a soul eating emotion."
— Carl Gustav Jung

About five years into my ministry, we adopted a second Vizsla. Debbie and Jeff's dog, Bella, passed away suddenly. We were all devastated when Bella died, so I talked Debbie into coming with me to visit some puppies.

"We'll just look," I lied.

In the middle of a rare Southern California rainstorm, Debbie and I drove to a farm in Ventura County and played with a pile of squirming Vizsla puppies. Afterwards, we went to a Chinese restaurant for lunch. We ended the meal with fortune cookies.

"Whatever is in these fortune cookies will determine our fate," I said. "The cookies will tell us whether or not we should *each* get a Vizsla puppy."

Our fortunes were something like, "Your path to success will be fulfilling," or "Patience is your ally."

"That's it," I said. "It's a sign."

"You think?" Debbie asked.

"Absolutely. We're getting puppies."

Hugh and I brought our second Vizsla home a few weeks later to be Stella's little brother. We named him Bartók—a Hungarian

Pointer named after the Hungarian composer, Béla Bartók—and we called him Bartie for short. Bartie was a typical puppy who tormented us with abundant chewing, barking, burrowing under the covers, and an overwhelming need to exercise. We loved him dearly.

Baby Bartie

One day, I took Bartie to the beach to meet some friends and their dogs. Our pup wrestled with his pals and raced after seagulls, intoxicated with the joy of running. Like most Vizsla puppies, he loved to chase birds.

Suddenly, Bartie became hyper-alert. An enormous pelican rested at the edge of the waves. Bartie bounded toward the bird, and it rose from the surf like a stealth jet, casting a shadow on the sand as it flew. Rather than focusing on the pelican, Bartie chased the bird's shadow. He bounded down the beach at high speed, red puppy legs flailing, tongue hanging out, and ears flapping beside him. Then the bird's shadow was gone. Bartie ran so fast, he outran the shadow. The shadow was behind him and there was nothing to chase. Bartie seemed bewildered by the absence of the shadow for a moment. Then he shook the ocean water off of his fur coat and bounded away to celebrate life on another patch of sand.

It's as if Bartie said, "Get thee behind me, shadow!" I wondered: *Could I do the same?*

The church and I were doing much better, but I still experienced an inner struggle with ministry. I had all this spiritual training that was supposed to "fix" me. But some of it just didn't seem to take. I thought, *Maybe I'm caught in an unexamined shadow. Maybe I need to be like Bartie and get ahead of whatever this shadow is. And maybe the process can be as effortless and as joyful as a dog running on the beach.*

Once again, I was bewitched by the power of paradox. It seemed to me the only way I could get out in front of my shadow was to draw closer to it. When every part of me wanted to push my shadow away, I realized I had to befriend it, to examine it with curiosity and compassion.

I looked within and saw that although the circumstances in my life kept changing, the insecurities I experienced remained similar. Whether I was engaged in acting, singing, or ministry, I felt the need to prove myself. Wherever I went, there I was. Against every new backdrop, I believed I was somehow fundamentally inadequate to the tasks at hand. I believed my inadequacy would invoke colossal rejection.

I began to suspect that shame was the source of my shadow. Brené Brown writes: "Shame is that warm feeling that washes over us making us feel small, flawed, and never good enough…" Her words offered me a familiar mirror and I didn't like it. The shame shadow was hard to see because it felt ugly. I wanted a classier shadow, something more acceptable. I was ashamed of my shame.

When I found the courage to confess my shame and examine it, I could see it was like a boa constrictor, squeezing the joy and freedom out of my ministry and my life. I couldn't ignore it any longer. I had to take the snake out of the driver's seat and put it behind me—while still allowing the snake to stay in the car. I couldn't run over the snake and kill it. I couldn't banish shame completely. Because even our shameful shame belongs in the kingdom of heaven on earth.

Reflections

Head: What is your shadow? Do you struggle with shame?

Heart: Divine Love, help me to see my shadow with compassion.

Hands: Practice curiosity with your shadow. Ask it questions and listen with respect. Take the shadow out of the driver's seat—but keep it in the car.

THE SOURCE OF SHAME

"We live in an atmosphere of shame. We are ashamed of everything that is real about us; ashamed of ourselves, of our relatives, of our incomes, of our accents, of our opinion, of our experience, just as we are ashamed of our naked skins."

—George Bernard Shaw

I began to usher the constrictor of shame out of the driver's seat by looking at how it slithered behind the wheel in the first place. I looked for the source of my shame. Most people look to their family of origin. So did I.

My parents were wonderful and well-meaning. They wanted us to excel in life, so they held us to high standards. In their all-too-human efforts to grow successful children, I'm sure they infected us with perfectionism. Thus, I was raised in a family of competitive overachievers. Part of me believed I would only be loved if I met certain conditions. My acceptability and belonging felt conditional. I was sure I would feel cast out and ashamed if I failed socially, academically, musically, morally, and more.

Comparison also impacted my shame-level. I am the youngest of four daughters. My sisters seemed smarter and more skilled than me simply because they were older. I was no slouch; plus, I compensated by being the cute, curly-headed, comical baby of the family. Still, in many ways I expected to be compared—and found inadequate—next to my older, more accomplished sisters.

Once when I was around five years old, I figuratively splattered my shame on our living room wallpaper like mustard-colored wet paint. In my family, we learned to read music as soon as we learned to read words. I created some compositions on the piano and my sisters asked to hear them. I played my first song perfectly, struck the last note, and immediately started booing myself. Why? Because I expected my big sisters to make fun of me. My sisters were bewildered by the booing. They liked my little songs—but still I felt a need to reject myself before anyone else could.

The Hess Sisters' Christmas - Nancy, Bonnie, Judy, Carol.

This shameful self-rejecting behavior followed me into the church. My self-rejector was the one who reacted when people criticized my clothes. My shame-fueled perfectionism was why a poorly received sermon felt humiliating. My toxic need for approval was why losing congregants felt like death. At the time, I didn't know I could simply shake all of this off like a wet dog flinging sand and saltwater at the beach. The little girl who booed her own piano compositions was alive and well, inwardly booing herself in a church.

Then there's religion. I grew up in a gentle Christian church with little hellfire, sin, and damnation. Yet somehow I picked up a notion from the prevailing culture that God has a mean streak. Despite years of metaphysical training about a God of love, I still carried a small yet persistent nag that if I erred, I would wind up on God's shit-list. God would frown upon me and banish me.

When I joined my current denomination, I was taught to affirm, "I am whole, perfect, and complete." I didn't have good definitions of those words at the time. So my ego said, *"Really? I am? Well thank you for noticing!"* Then I strove to uphold my ego's definition of "whole, perfect, and complete," again trying to achieve myself into acceptability.

In metaphysical teachings, sometimes the ego takes hold, and we develop a second shadow that covers shame with a ghostly illusion of spirituality. Our fellow travelers on a spiritual path become new targets for comparison. We try to be as spiritual as others to prove our acceptability. But the shadow of trying to "be more spiritual" wrestles with the shadow of shame—and the wrestling match drags us into a deeper pit.

Dr. Martin Luther King said, "Hate cannot drive out hate," and "Darkness cannot drive out darkness." The same is true for the shadow and shame. Shadow cannot drive out shame. Shame cannot drive out shadow. When we attempt to fix a shadow with a shadow, we either fail outright; or we fail by false success—in other words, we *think* we conquer the shadow, but really we just temporarily contain it. We cram a roiling stew of shadow into a tight Tupperware. We seal the lid and stick it in storage. Suppression invites the shadow to ferment and eventually explode into a pseudo-poltergeist that interferes with the fullness of life.

I know for me, when my ego was in charge—if I ever had moments of brokenness, imperfection, or incompletion—I pressed myself into the metaphorical Tupperware with gusto. I would not allow the power of a negative thought. I prayed my tank-like prayers to invoke outer symbols of success. I believed if I could just apply enough evidentiary band-aids to fasten my life together, then people would think I was okay. They would think I was "doing it right," that I was truly as "whole, perfect, and complete" as all the really gifted spiritual people were. If I could just get other people to accept me, then maybe I could accept myself. I worked hard at acceptability and was fairly successful—that is until the shame-filled Tupperware exploded again, and I found myself wiping up a mess of pain with a self-rejecting ego.

Eventually I entered into a mystical, non-dual path and learned new definitions of "whole, perfect, and complete." Wholeness includes brokenness; perfect literally means inclusive of everything; complete means evolving. I incorporated this paradoxical wisdom into my life and became gentler with myself and others.

Richard Rohr says, "What you do not transform, you will transmit." I looked at my life and compassionately observed my transmittal of suppressed shame. My transmittal took many forms—hypersensitivity, eye-rolling, defensiveness, and criticism of self and others. My heightened awareness of transmitted shame brought me to a new place of paradox and willingness.

I was willing to see how the shame-inducing ego is part of

love's plan, but not in the way I thought it was. Shame doesn't exist to make us smaller; it exists to call us to inner greatness through humility. We acknowledge shame. We befriend our humanity and offer it compassion. Our compassion inspires us to regard ourselves unconditionally. Then we transcend our imagined limits of acceptability through the powers of grace, forgiveness, and love. In other words, we *love ourselves beyond our capacity to love ourselves. We learn to let God love through us. This lovingness extends to our love for others as well.*

Is there a checklist that describes the methodology used to transcend shame? Is there a to-do list for invoking unconditional acceptance through grace, forgiveness, and love? I don't think so. The path is an individual process designed by God. Our life is our to-do list, as well as our to-be list. That's how it was for me.

My inner work led me to trust in something greater than myself. My trust allowed willingness, and willingness gave me insight—a clearer intellectual understanding of my soul's journey. However, living beings need experience. If you read a book about swimming, it's not the same as getting in the water and moving your body. The same theory applies to embracing and transcending shame. You can read about it all you want, but you won't understand shame until you thrash around in the cesspool for a while.

God graciously provided me with an experience to supplement my intellectual understanding of shame. Sadly, it wasn't a visitation from an angel chorus singing a medley of answers to all my questions. God did not unfurl a heavenly banner that said, "You are loved just as you are." No, God in her great wit provided me with a shameful experience—one where I could writhe acutely and heal abundantly.

A beloved congregant was dying of a rapidly progressing illness. His Christian brother lurked near the death bed, where he observed my prayers and gasped in dismay at his perception of my inadequacy. Through his lens, I failed to minister to the dying man because I did not ask him to profess his allegiance to Christ. It's not part of our theology. We bless all paths to God and trust that everyone who dies goes home to a good afterlife. Like everything else, the afterlife is perfect. Inclusive of everyone.

I could feel our congregant's brother waiting for me to leave so he could offer salvation in the name of sweet Jesus. I went out to get some food. When I returned, the dying congregant was sitting up in his bed. He said, "My Christian brother prayed for me. There's been a conversion. I think I'm going to pull through."

Later I relayed this story to a minister colleague.

"Dammit, why does that Christian guy get all the credit? I mean, what's wrong with *my* prayers?" I said. "Okay, the sick guy ended up dying anyway, but all the same, if there was a Jesus-level healing upgrade, I wanted it to come from *me*."

Right there, I was immersed in the shadows of shame and inadequacy, manifesting as the need for unwarranted control, approval, and pride. My colleague smirked at me and said, "Yes… because it *is* all about you, Bonnie, isn't it?"

I got it. My colleague's arch comment was an invitation to see anew. I saw how control, approval, perfectionism, and pride were all false gods. My shame chased after these false gods like they were made of chocolate chip cookie dough. I was caught in a festering cycle of using a shadow to drive out a shadow. I knew there had to be a better way. I didn't know what it was, but I was willing to learn.

Reflections

Head: If you experience shame, what do you perceive as the source of it?

Heart: Divine Love, help me remember you have never been ashamed of me. Help me celebrate myself as I am.

Hands: Practice radical forgiveness of self and others.

LOVING THE SHADOW INTO LIGHT

"The truth is hidden because it's so bright."
—Ibn Arabi

My experience in the church deepened and my ministry moved from hapless to happy. When people ask, "What did you do to change things?" I usually say, "I'm not sure…the changes were almost indiscernible. I didn't make any major outer changes. I didn't come up with a new strategic plan. I didn't enroll in a class on how to eliminate eye-rolling. All I know is I changed on the inside—and then the outsides followed."

I continued to work with my shadow of shame. I relaxed just a little. As I did, I witnessed my addiction to chasing the shadow of shame and inched toward a gentler way. I started asking more internal questions: *What would happen if I welcomed every aspect of my being? Can I accept my shadowy shame as I would a lonely, frightened child?*

I could. It started with honesty about what I was feeling. I was ashamed. For once, I didn't try and pimp-slap the shame away with spiritual self-help. I didn't bellow affirmations such as, "I am completely free of all shame right now!" Instead, I said, "I am no longer ashamed of my shame."

Bonnie, age 15 months.

That affirmation became true immediately. When I gave myself permission to feel my shame—to release shame around my shame—there was no waiting for the affirmation to "work." The affirmation itself was answered prayer. Plus, when I was no longer ashamed of my shame, the shame didn't seem like "my" shame anymore. It felt like a small beam of light in the prism of the human condition. It was everybody's shame, just part of living on planet earth. When I stopped empowering shame with personal ownership, it began to dissipate. It returned to the native nothingness from where it came.

The way to stop chasing the shadow is to stop chasing the shadow. Stop chasing and let God be God. Let the truth be true. Stop chasing the shadow and turn toward the light—not because of what the light can offer us—but because it is so bright.

Shame is nothing. The shadow is nothing. It is an illusion created and empowered by another illusion, the illusion of a separate self. Beneath all the fretting, worrying, self-doubt and fear; behind every perception of failure and inadequacy; behind every scramble to get it right, a true self embraces and transcends all the images we chase. This self is humble, glorious, and universal. The true self is happiness and peace. It smiles at our attachment to shame, self-importance, pride, and humiliation. It shakes its non-head when we judge ourselves and others. It all but slaps its non-existent knee and guffaws when we engage in a "prayerful" competition to try and take credit for healing a dying congregant. It helps us remember true prayer is about getting out of the way so love can work through us.

Welcoming the shadow aligns us with the true self. Welcoming shakes off the resistance that causes the shadow to both hide and fight harder. Welcoming allows perfection, meaning inclusion. When we welcome the shadow, we turn toward the light and open like rosebuds in the spring. Then the light teaches us.

The light teaches us every time we catch ourselves needlessly seeking approval, we can relax and remember the true self is impervious to the twin seductions of praise and blame.

The light teaches us if we disappoint someone, the disappointment of others often does not belong to us. If we have truly let someone down we apologize and make amends. If we are innocent, we see the disappointment belongs to the disappointed. In the glory of the true self, we strip disappointment of its power and see it as nothing.

The light teaches us there are no mistakes, only patterns of grace unfolding. If we quiet our busy minds and step back just a little, we can trust life's ever-inclusive patterns.

The light teaches us to take things lightly—to laugh at perceived mistakes and celebrate the comedy of being human.

The light leads us to abide in the presence as the presence, beyond necessary opposites such as success and failure. In the light, success and failure "belong to the beloved."[16]

The light teaches us that the process matters more than the prize. It teaches us to detach from outcomes and refrain from taking credit. Our prayers, intentions, actions, and outcomes all flow from an eternal source. We remember, get out of the way, and allow the I Am presence to prevail.[17]

The light teaches us forgiveness for self and others. It reminds us erring is part of perfection. And healing is hard—but only because the truth is too beautiful to behold.

Then the light floods us with paradox. It contradicts itself

---

[16] From a poem by Rumi: "I belong to the beloved, have seen the two worlds as one..."

[17] I Am is a name for God. God (Spirit) creates matter out of itself, and we, the I Am, are individual expressions of God. "The highest God and the innermost God is one God." (Ernest Holmes).

and reminds us healing is ridiculously easy when we open our eyes to omnipresent grace.

The light teaches us that God banishes no one. God doesn't have a shit-list. God is a boundless arena of infinite good. There cannot be a boundless arena of infinite good and someplace else. There cannot be a realm of banishment that exists outside of God. If there is only God, there is nowhere to go but God.

The light teaches us that the shadow falls behind us when we disempower it. It is an illusion with zero influence in the presence of the true self.

But also, when we put the shadow behind us, it takes on new meaning. It has our backs. It is behind us to support us by inviting us to see it with compassion so we may experience the exultation of new growth through an assertion of boundless love.

The layers of paradox in shadow and light may be bewildering at first. But if we watch and pray, we become like Bartie, chasing the shadow of a majestic bird. Pursuit becomes play in the fields of unconditional joy. Then, when we outrun the shadow, the light inspires us to frolic onward, to play on an ever-available brighter patch of sand. Undoubtedly, there will be shadows to chase there, too—but once we've embraced and transcended one shadow, we can embrace and transcend them all.

Reflections

Head: What does the light teach you?

Heart: Divine Love, help me to say, "I am no longer ashamed of my shame."

Hands: Talk to yourself and others as you would relate to a precious child (or pet).

PUTTING THE FUN IN FUNERAL

"Someone who knows God has dropped the cruel knife that most so often use upon their tender self and others."
—Hāfez

When I first started at the church, I arrived as insatiable insecurity incarnate—an over-zealous ego determined to prove my ability to succeed. How much wiser it would have been to begin ministry in the spirit of selfless service. To show up on my first day empty of ego and full of love. To recognize the shadows inherent in human life, but to use the shadow to inspire greater God-light. To ask spirit to transform my authentic strengths and weaknesses into serving the greatest good. To question, again and again, "How can I help," or "God, what do you need from me right now?"

A hidden part of me longed to live in a deeper relationship with surrendered service. As I mentioned before, I wanted to usher the shame-filled ego out of the driver's seat. But I didn't yet see how selfless service could actually help me transcend shame. And even when I began to have inklings of the humble empowerment gained by giving oneself away, I didn't know how to turn this theory into practice. The path of mystical transformation is beyond the logic of the ego. So because I didn't understand exactly *how* to transform, again God stepped in to steer me through another mortifying scenario.

It happened at a funeral. One of my ministerial colleagues passed away after a good long life. Her church requested we hold the memorial in our space because they expected a big crowd, and we have a large seating capacity.

Our denomination is known for providing kick-butt funerals. There is rarely weeping and wailing and gnashing of teeth. Although we provide space for grief, much of our focus is on celebrating life. I've seen it time and time again. Families come to me in distress. They feel the magnitude of honoring their loved one, the impossibility of capturing someone's significance in an hour-long service. I always smile and say, "You'll be surprised. Something magical happens. The good intentions in the room take over and everything unfolds according to love's plan."

I often arrive at funerals with happy, bouncy energy. I look forward to learning more about the deceased person through the stories people will tell. I look forward to swimming in the sea of love that will emerge. Our volunteers are like me, prone to revel in the joy of serving a family in a sacred time of passage. The volunteers' joy enhances my joy.

There have been times when I've felt so happy prior to a funeral, I'm afraid I'll be perceived as disrespectful. I don't mean to be. I'm joyful because I anticipate grace in our shared funereal journey. Still, occasionally pre-service, I'll take a prayer practitioner aside and say, "Will you please pray for me? Please ask God to help me tone down the joy a little. I'm putting too much fun in this funeral."

The funeral for my ministerial colleague was different. I was still relatively new at ministry. It was only my third funeral, and

I knew there would be lots of ministers speaking on behalf of the deceased. I compared myself to the other, more experienced ministers, and wondered if I would measure up. Again, a nagging voice yakked in my head about my skill or lack there-of.

We did the service and when it was over, I wanted validation. I needed people to ease my perception of inadequacy. At a funeral. I wasn't asking for a lot. I didn't need anyone to say, "Oh my God, Reverend Bonnie, your spiritual message put memorials on the map…Girl, you put the fun in funeral." A mere compliment, even a tiny "not bad," would have sufficed. Yet, no one praised me.

I started to berate myself for the neediness of wanting praise, and then berate myself some more for the embarrassment of not getting it. Then more berating for making it all about me. Again. At a funeral. Then wondering if maybe I had done something wrong in the service. All kinds of mental chatter cluttered my consciousness. Finally a new thought broke through: *Why don't you give what you would like to receive?*

I went up to every speaker and sincerely thanked them for participating. I was specific about how their words touched me. I did so without any expectation of return praise. I don't recall if anyone returned my compliments because it didn't matter. What I learned from this practice was more important than any fleeting words of praise could ever be.

I became the energy of unconditional reciprocity. The parallel virtues of giving and receiving became one as they moved through my body, mind, and spirit. Giving the gift of praise was all I needed to receive. I learned setting my ego aside and shifting from "what can I get" to "what can I give" changes everything. Again, I found the fun in a funeral—but this time in a way that shifted my consciousness toward *exponential* good.

Because now I get to bring this principle beyond funerals to the sacred-mundane tasks of living. I bring this practice to the grocery store, where I hold the intention to serve as I shop. I help short people reach items on high shelves. I help elderly folks find their favorite can of soup.

I bring the oneness of giving and receiving to Starbucks, where I talk with the baristas. I greet a young woman from India, who is eager to talk about her Sikh faith with me; and Daniel, who is training to be an EMT. Daniel tells me he "just wants someone to believe in him," and I say, "I know you can do it, my friend. Just look at how you sling those lattes."

I bring giving and receiving to a local restaurant where I bow to the waitress who wears killer false eyelashes. I tell her, "I can't put those things on without gluing my eye shut. Will you teach me?" I listen, I encourage, I laugh, and I allow. Always, without fail, I receive something wonderful when I give myself away.

Giving what we wish to receive is a superpower that blesses everyone. The benefits are priceless. When we show up with the intention to give, we serve from the true self. We align with the holiness that springs to life through sincere and generous circulation. For when the ego clings to nothing, we receive everything. When we decide to love without conditions, there is more to love. I wish I had known this on my first day of serving in a church. But I know it now, and that is enough.

Reflections

Head: What is missing from your life? What would you like to receive?

Heart: Divine Love, immerse me in the joy of giving what I wish to receive.

Hands: Practice giving what you would like to receive. Notice how this action changes you.

15

THE REVENGE OF THE NAKED BURRITO

"Your life within God's arms, Your dance within God's arms, Is already Perfect!"

—Hāfez

It took several years, but eventually *The Church of the Corn* became a center of love, a place where today we aspire to "Be Love, Share Love, and Serve Love." There were many changes. People who didn't resonate with my message left. The community worked together to gather new members. The finances stabilized and the spiritual teachings deepened. Becky moved away to Texas to take care of her aging mother. The Mexican restaurant removed The Naked Burrito from the menu. Eventually, the handsome cashier moved on as well. I continued to go there for lunch from time to time, even though it wasn't the same without Becky and our cashier.

One Sunday after a dynamic morning at church, I ordered a take-out tofu veggie burrito. Two days later, I noticed bright red numbers in my online checking account—copious over-draft fees. The person who took my order activated a system error and charged me $49,000. For a burrito.

I was a bit perplexed, but rather than make up dire tales of bankruptcy invoked by the revenge of the anti-naked-burrito (the karma of my former impure thoughts) I trusted and acted.

I called the restaurant.

"It was a delicious burrito," I said. "But I don't think it was worth $49,000, do you?"

The young woman on the phone laughed and said, "We will fix this for you. Here's the manager's cell number. He'll take care of you."

When I called, I recognized the man's voice. It was the handsome cashier with the pectorals.

I chuckled as I realized I was past my old-lady crush. I congratulated him on his promotion to manager and joked about my costly lunch.

"Does this mean I own a franchise now?" I asked.

"I'm afraid not," he said. "But I'll reverse the charges and give you lots of store credit. That'll keep you eating my burritos for a while."

I didn't even blush at the thought of eating his burritos. I hung up the phone completely awestruck.

I was no longer infatuated with naked burrito guy. I was infatuated with God—God as a glorious process with a wild sense of humor. God who orchestrated a $49,000 burrito. I saw God's sweet indulgence through the early years of ministry, tripping me, throwing humiliation-pies in my face, pushing me into slapstick opportunities to grow. It was a cosmic sit-com where anything could happen. And everything made sense in the hindsight of divine wisdom and wit.

My congregation today doesn't like hearing about how the church was for me back then. They don't like the term, *The Church of the Corn*, and who can blame them? I call it that because it makes me laugh. Then I reassure them *The Church of the Corn* was never about them. The church's challenges were reflections of my own insecurities rising to be seen and healed. The people who stayed, the people who left, the people who criticized me—all were divine gifts offered to this grossly inexperienced minister who vainly attempted to stake her claim and find her authentic right to be there.

Why did I stay, even when it was so hard?

Back in the corn years, every day I asked myself, *Are you happy?* I always heard my still small voice say, *Yes.*

There was a lot of humor mixed in with the humiliation. Plus, I intuited the process of bringing shadow into light as a path of incredible growth. Each incremental step in the journey brought me eventual joy.

Then there's love. With fingers crossed, hoping God would give me a ticket out of the hapless church, every day I also asked, *Should I stay?* Again, I heard, *Yes.*

Love said, *Stay.* When I tried to argue with that answer, a vision of our dog, Stella, pawed at my consciousness like she was burrowing in a blanket to get under the covers. God gave me our church through Stella. Once I arrived, God used Stella like super-glue to hold me there. After all, Stella loved to run on the beach. In God's view, that was reason enough to remain.

On the unseen side of life, God knew if I stayed, love would eventually reach me and teach me. Like my rambunctious Vizslas, I needed a little extra support in learning how to stay. So in the early years of *The Church of the Corn*, love anchored me in place with Stella. God used our pointer-dog to give me the grace to sit, stay, and eventually heal.

Reflections

Head: Go deep and ask, "Where is love trying to reach me and teach me?"

Heart: Divine Love, help me trust the perfection of your plan.

Hands: Throughout the day, ask yourself, "Am I happy?" Place something in your home, car, or other to remind you that happiness is your true nature.

*The Ventura Center for Spiritual Living, www.venturacsl.org.
Photo by Loren Alan.*

PART THREE:

DANCES WITH CANCER

LOOKING FOR SIGNS

"When suffering comes, we yearn for some sign from God, forgetting we have just had one."
—Mignon McLaughlin

With all the revelations I just described, one might think I would be complete in my healing. Wrong. As I said before, completion is evolution. Completion in God is an ongoing process. Still, I was surprised when Hugh gave me an affectionate squeeze one morning, and it turned into a breast exam. He guided my hand to the spot, and there it was—a lump designed to change my destiny. It had been a decade since my last mammogram.

I knew better. My mother died of breast cancer when I was a teenager. Two of my sisters survived cancer in their 40s. I worked as a nurse at Sloane Kettering Cancer Center in New York. But I avoided breast exams and mammograms for a convoluted host of reasons: *The doctor will be mad at me for waiting so long. They might find something. I don't want to know.*

Most of all, I didn't think it could happen to me. When we found the lump I told Hugh, "It's probably nothing. I'm not a cancer-y kind of person." Then we scattered to our separate laptops where we could fix the situation with information.

Hugh googled ways I may have attacked my immune system

with food and devised a plot to force-feed me health-boosting vegetables. He ordered an emulsifier blender to grind kale and other cancer fighters into a smoothie I could drink daily.

"You will take care of this, won't you?" he said. "You're not going to be all nurse-like and ignore this, right?"

"I'll see a doctor and I'll be fine," I promised. "Even if I'm not fine, I will be fine."

That seemed like a brave thing to say. For a moment, I saw myself as an operatic heroine, say Violetta in *La Traviata*, stricken with a fatal illness yet still singing her guts out right before she dies onstage. So even if it was cancer, I could inspire others with a noble, soul-stirring death. I felt good about that. Then I got back on the internet and prayed to Google: *Give me a sign this will be okay.*

My Google search started an avalanche of worst-case scenario spam. I got breast prosthesis-spammed as the internet predicted bi-lateral mastectomies. I was wig-spammed as the internet assumed hair loss from chemo.

When I received an advertisement from a discount design-your-own-coffin emporium featuring a bouquet of satin coffin linings, I said to myself, *The turquoise is on my Color Me Beautiful palette. It will look good with my eyes...But still, God, give me a sign.*

Then our rabbit, Romeo, slipped into a coma.

Romeo was a small brown rabbit I viewed as a symbol of Shakespearean love. One day he was hopping around in search of his next romance. The next day he was comatose on the floor of his pen, a barely breathing fur ball in a pile of hay. He seemed pain-free. He was ancient and it was time. So we decided to let him go in his own way—no drastic measures, just keep him comfortable.

Why now? Rabbits represent life and fertility. Romeo's goal was to copulate with his littermate, Julius, with our cat, and with my fuzzy pink slipper. When his life began to seep into the hay, I wondered if my robust life would drain away, too. Did death send me a telegram in the form of a dying Romeo? Was this my sign?

I kept going. Every day I made Hugh's disgusting green drink, which behaved more like a bovine cud than a beverage. I checked the rabbit and searched the internet. I looked in the mirror and imagined myself bald from chemo.

I hunted for my old red nursing stethoscope so I could listen for cancer in my lungs. I checked the lump every hour or so to see if it had gone away yet. I did crazy math to calculate the odds. *This will be benign*, I told myself. *Cancer affects one in eight women; there are five people in my book club, and Ellen got it, so that means it won't happen to me.*

I hiked with the dogs and ran the church and didn't tell anyone what was happening. Then I took Hugh's advice and made an appointment with a doctor.

The nurse led me to the exam room where I put on a limp hospital gown. To quiet my racing mind, I reached for a pamphlet in the exam room. The title on the pamphlet was, "Bonnie Struggles with Incontinence."

Seriously? Of all the names in the world available for your basic incontinence brochure, they had to pick my name? Was this a sign? Soon I would be peeing in my pants? Soon I would lose control of everything dear to me, including my bladder?

It turned out the brochure was about Bonnie Blair, an Olympic speed skater, who "broke the ice about incontinence."

The doctor arrived, cheery and chatting about hiking as she pressed my breasts. I made jokes, striving for a blasé approach to cancer.

"I'm not worried, but my *husband* is," I told her.

She told me to relax and made an appointment for a mammogram. I went home and checked the internet to see why Bonnie Blair was wetting herself. Stress incontinence, Google said.

The next day, I got up, chewed my cud, and checked the rabbit. He was still alive, but still dying. Then I went to get a mammogram.

Having a mammogram is like inviting a horse to step on your breasts. Still, I decided, *I can have fun with this.* Our young dog, Bartie the shadow-chaser, needed lots of exercise, so I loaded him into the car. I promised Bartie, "I'll just zip in, let the horse trample my bosoms, and then we'll go to the dog park."

The mammogram took much longer than anticipated. Was this a sign? I worried about Bartie overheating in the car. After an hour, I wanted to ask for a break to check on him. I felt guilty about disturbing the radiologist's routine, afraid she would wonder what kind of a fool brings her dog to a mammogram.

You care too much what other people think, I said to myself. *You're a big people pleaser, and that's maybe why you caught cancer.* So I stopped the radiologist and the technician and asked for permission to leave. When they said no, I insisted. I put on my clothes and moved the car to the indoor parking garage, where I knew Bartie would be safe.

I came back and they continued the breast pummeling. The radiologist was disgruntled because I left.

"I'm new at this," I said apologetically. "I didn't know the mammogram would take so long…and I would never forgive myself if my dog got overheated and died because I was afraid of your white coat."

I said it politely but firmly and the radiologist nodded like she understood. At the end of the exam, the radiologist told me they found some suspicious areas on the mammogram and asked me to come back for needle biopsies. Was this a sign?

At the start of the cancer journey, I did what humans do. I

prayed for a sign that everything would all be right. I hoped for skywriting, or at the very least, a post-it on my bathroom mirror. When that didn't happen, I looked for signs that something was wrong.

A *Color Me Beautiful* coffin lining, a dying rabbit, and an incontinent speed skater. In hindsight, these are not objective signs of impending death. Even though I caught rare glimpses that everything would work out, my fear turned visible happenings into evidence of virulent cancer. As usual, I felt the need to appear calm and stoic. "Don't let them see you sweat," was my motto. But beneath my semi-serene exterior, a reality of fear took hold, leaving little room for faith.

Reflections

Head: Where are you looking for signs from God?

Heart: Divine Love, help me bring inner peace to all outer signs.

Hands: Offer encouragement to someone in distress. Be a sign of goodwill for others.

THE DAY THE RABBIT DIED

"Parting is such sweet sorrow."
—Shakespeare, Romeo and Juliet

I had my needle biopsies, took Bartie to the dog park, and returned home to check the rabbit. Romeo was dead. He died during my biopsies. *This has got to be a sign*, my brain said.

Hugh was out of town working, so I dug Romeo's grave. I chose a secluded area in our back yard. The ground was hard, I had a headache, and my chest was sore. My body was a traitor, too pathetic for grave digging—but short of sticking my dead rabbit in the freezer next to the Lean Cuisines, I didn't know what else to do. So I hacked at the earth with a shovel and made a hole. I knew it was too shallow. But it was the best I could do.

I tried to make amends, jazz it up a little to atone for the lack of depth and for my weakness. I thought about those *Color Me Beautiful* coffin linings, and placed a layer of soft pink rose petals in the hole. *Romeo's brown coat looks good in pink*, I thought.

I placed Romeo's body in the grave with a carrot beside him. Then I straightened his silky ears and thanked him for being our bunny. I only cried a little. I was in too much pain and afraid if I started crying, I wouldn't be able to stop.

It's always hard to throw dirt over an animal when you've

spent a decade keeping them safe. I felt the tug of wanting Romeo to be comfortable, to be able to breathe, even though breath was no longer an option. I scooped the soil gently and covered his face last. Bit by bit, our bunny disappeared under an impersonal layer of dirt. I wished the hole was deeper, but it wasn't, so I rolled a stone over the grave and hoped for the best.

Romeo rose on the third day, but not in a good way. This was no Easter Sunday celebration.

As I googled stage-four metastases on the computer, Stella and Bartie—A.K.A. Cujo and Satan—bounded into my home office. They attempted to squeeze their 50-pound bodies under the armchair cushions. They avoided eye contact and their ears drooped. These are all signs of Vizsla guilt. They also exuded a soul-crushing stench of death.

Guilty dogs - Stella and Bartok.

My heart crashed. "Fuck me," I said in despair. I knew what the evil ones had done.

Through sheer willpower, I dragged myself to the backyard cemetery and fell to my knees in front of the gaping hole where Romeo used to be. The heathen-dogs had rolled away the stone. Then the little shits dug out the decomposing bunny, rolled in him, tore him up, and threw pieces of the wreckage all around the backyard. They even ate the damn carrot. There was no resurrection in this, and the shadow of death loomed larger.

Hugh came home that evening and re-buried the dismembered Romeo, kindly and efficiently. Then one day post rabbit-exhumation, I got the news.

I was in my office at the church when my cell phone rang. My doctor and I both paused, like we were waiting at the intersection at a four-way stop sign, to see who would go first. Finally I said, "Just tell me."

"It's treatable," she said, "but you have cancer."

I didn't know what to think. As a former nurse, who once worked in a major cancer hospital, I knew what could happen. Plus, the internet told me I would lose body parts, my hair, and my life. So I began thinking about the stages and spread. Surely the worst scenario couldn't happen to me. I mean, I did half-bury my rabbit and bring a dog to my mammogram; but am I really the type of person to catch cancer? Seriously, it couldn't happen to me.

At the same time, I was sure it was cancer, bad cancer. Every twitch was evidence of fire-breathing malignancy. I stayed up late, under a blanket on the couch, squashed between the two rabbit-exhuming dogs, watching re-runs of *House*, finding hope in television's undiagnosed illnesses. *That person getting diagnosed by the grumpy Dr. House is worse off than me*, I thought. Then I wondered if the stabbing pain in my hip meant the cancer had spread. Or maybe it was just a dog toenail digging in.

Reflections

Head: How does uncertainty affect your life?

Heart: Divine Love, please help me find comfort in uncertainty.

Hands: If you are concerned about something, act as necessary; then let go it for a while. Participate in a completely unrelated activity and see what happens.

THE CONE OF SHAME

"Cancer is probably the unfunniest thing in the world, but I'm a comedian, and even cancer couldn't stop me from seeing the humor in what I went through."
—Gilda Radner

I told the church leaders about the cancer two days before I had surgery, just in case I croaked in the operating room. I wanted them to pray for me. About nine days after the surgery, I had to tell the rest of the congregation. This could be problematic.

Our teaching suggests we create the things that happen to us. Many people use this theory as a weapon. We judge ourselves and others for "creating" our illnesses. We do so to give the illusion of control saying, "If I created it, I can un-create it." Or, "If I just think the right thoughts, nothing bad will ever happen to me."

Sometimes there is a linear cause and effect relationship between thoughts, actions, and outcomes. Certainly, if we play in traffic, we could get run over. If we eat like fools, we're likely to gain weight or get a food-related illness, such as hypertension.

My minister friend, Marc, asks his congregation to consider Jesus. Some serious junk happened to Jesus, but no one stood at the foot of the cross asking, "Jesus, what was in your consciousness? How did you create this crucifixion business?"

"Bad" things happen. While we always have a choice about our reactions to life, we don't always know why things occur as they do. Life is a mystery. Yet I was nervous about telling my congregation about my diagnosis. I was afraid they would judge me for having "cancer consciousness."

I arrived at the church that morning, nine days post-op, and met with the leaders for our usual pre-service prayer. They circled me like bomb-sniffing dogs. Their empathy was palpable, but I could tell they were worried, avoiding saying the wrong thing and wondering who I was, now that I had the cancer and all. Our pre-service prayer circle usually contains a lot of comedy, but that Sunday, it was quiet like a mortuary.

Our office manager, Annette, assigned the Sunday tasks to the volunteers. Then she reminded everyone I needed a hug-free-zone. No hugs that might press sutured flesh and rip out radiation catheters. The volunteers paused to contemplate that news. Perhaps they visualized a hugging frenzy—and the energy in the room shifted. The circle revved their comedy engines. There was an accelerando of goodwill, imitating football blocks and wrestling strategies to protect me from over-zealous huggers in the congregation.

Then Judy Rogers, a practitioner, said, "I know! Let's put one of those dog-head-cones on her boob."

I visualized an enormous plastic dog-cone-of-shame applied to my chest. I saw myself entering the sanctuary preceded by my clear plastic dog cone and laughed out loud. The others laughed with me and something relaxed. The circle heaved a collective sigh and silently conveyed, *She hasn't changed. Everything will be okay. She hasn't lost her joy.*

The church service began and then it was time to tell our congregation. Inspired by our leadership team, I worked up to the cancer reveal with comedy. I wanted people to know it's okay to laugh, even with the scary cancer scratching at the stained-glass windows. I spoke to the congregation about the meanings we assign to words. I said, "There's a certain word in American culture. This word used to be normal. But now when you say it, it always gets a reaction."

"Is it gay?" an elderly gentleman yelped, three rows back.

"Good try!" I replied. "But no, the word I'm looking for is a gardening tool. It rhymes with 'toe'!"

Gino, a boisterous black gospel singer shot her hand up. She grunted and wiggled like an eager second grader. I called on her and she proudly said, "Ho. The word is ho." [18]

"That's right," I said. "Ho. Ho is just a collection of sounds. But look how much meaning we give it!"

I told about a time when I worked as a nurse in a mental health facility and participated in a staff and patient meeting. One of the therapists complained the patients were neglecting the therapy garden. "If you want a garden, you have to take care of it," the therapist admonished.

An ancient Mexican American man clacked his dentures and declared, "I'll help in the garden when you get me a hoe." When he said that, a tsunami of suppressed laughter strangled the circle. One of the nursing students raised her hand and asked, "How much does a ho cost nowadays?"

The congregation got the joke and they laughed and nodded. *Yes, we do apply meanings to words,* they seemed to say.

Still, they didn't know the secret I held. I didn't want to ruin their appreciation of my strange humor, but I had to. So I took a deep breath and told them about another word that wields power, a word that would swallow the room once I said it—and then I spoke it aloud.

---

[18] Based on a skit by Eddie Murphy on *Saturday Night Live*: Velvet Jones: I Wanna Be a Ho.

"Cancer. I have cancer."

The cancer cat was out of the bag. I asked them, "How will we define this word called cancer? How much power will we give it?"

Reflections

*Head: **Can you find the comedy in a difficult situation?***

*Heart: **Divine Love, teach me to laugh even when life is challenging.***

*Hands: **Throughout the day, step back from challenges and see if there is any room for joy.***

REDEFINING CANCER

"Cancer is a word, not a sentence."
—John Diamond

I told the congregation this story: I was scheduled to have a total of ten radiation treatments in five days. On day four, my nephew, David, called to ask if I wanted help. Hugh was working out of town, so David offered to drive to Ventura County from his home in Los Angeles and take me to radiation, cook for me, shop for me, and do whatever I needed. I told him I was a little tired but doing fine.

He assumed I was lying, trying to brave. "Are you being all stoic again?" he asked.

I laughed and said, "If you really want to help, come over and wear out the dogs."

Aside from the rabbit carcass incident, Stella and Bartie were missing their daily exercise routine. David put on his running clothes and drove to my home. He collected Stella and Bartie and ran several miles with them. While David ran with the dogs, I went to radiation treatment number eight. I was almost done.

I remembered my mother, who died of cancer when I was a teenager. She was brave and mostly cheerful throughout the entire journey. But she once made a passing comment: "The radiation department is the most depressing place in the world," she said. And I believed her. My mother said it, so it must be true.

I tested my mother's theory and discovered her reality about radiation didn't match mine. During treatment, I rested on the softest table imaginable and stared at a picture of cherry blossoms on the ceiling. A gentle radiologist hooked me up to a device that looked like *The Starship Enterprise*. As *The Enterprise* worked its magic, I remained in pristine stillness, wrapped in the music of Ella Fitzgerald and Frank Sinatra. After 20 minutes, a technician unhooked me. I got dressed and walked to the front desk where the office staff gave me candy. Then I went home to relax on the sofa with the dogs. I liked radiation.

The day my nephew came to help, I came back from my treatment, tired but happy to see him and grateful for the wearing-out he offered Stella and Bartie. David brought us Thai food for dinner. We ate together, laughing and chatting in the backyard.

When we finished eating, I went into the kitchen to clean up. As I rinsed dishes, *Baby Got Back* shuffled onto my music queue. I enjoy Sir Mix-a-Lot's homage to gigantic bottoms, so I started singing. "I like big butts and I cannot lie. You other brothers can't deny…" I shook my own substantial booty and danced as I loaded the dishwasher. David came up behind me, carrying the rest of the dinner plates. Suddenly, I sensed his presence. I turned around to smile at him and saw tears in his eyes.

"You really *are* okay," he said.

"Of course I am," I laughed. "I am redefining cancer."

My whole life, I told myself this illness couldn't happen to me as I secretly waited for the cancer shoe to fall and dropkick me through the goalpost of hell. Cancer was a scary word, too scary to face. That's why I didn't get mammograms for all those years. Even the possibility was too much to consider, so I denied it as long as I could.

Now I had a new story. I told the congregation about how coming down with a touch of cancer was more like coming up, coming up to something precious. Cancer was a gift. It was a revelation.

Shortly after my diagnosis, while pondering death, I thought, *If I die, at least I got to sing opera with an orchestra.* That thought inspired other thoughts, where I examined all the parts of my life. I saw that my whole life was a banquet of priceless experiences. Every detail was "wild and precious," to echo Mary Oliver. Everything was consummated by grace. Cancer gave me the eyes to see the kingdom of heaven in my life, *as* my life upon the earth.

I told all of this to the congregation, and they understood. Then I told them the other good news: The cancer was stage one. After a lumpectomy and ten radiation treatments, I would most likely survive.

The congregation clapped and I cried with joy.

I anticipated they might judge me. Maybe some did and maybe I still harbored a little judgment of myself, but the predominant feeling in the room was love. The church service ended, and people respected the hug-free-zone. Women came up to me and whispered, "I'm a 10-year survivor..." and "I'm a 23-year survivor..."

I decided to call myself a nine-day survivor. And that was that. To this day, the cancer has not returned.

My experience with cancer was a slow dance of love and learning. Adorned in the readiness to love my enemy, I parted the curtain to see what gifts she would offer. The gifts were infinite, shown in darkness and light, in sickness and in health, in a dead rabbit, and in naughty dogs. I saw the beloved for better and for worse in the ongoing mystical marriage of spirit in all. Cancer was a blessing that revealed the capacity for infinite good in everything. I would not change it.

Reflections

Head: Are there any difficult areas in your life that might benefit from re-definition?

Heart: Divine Love, teach me to see the good in everything.

Hands: Offer someone (if they are willing) a new perspective on a challenging issue.

THE PURPOSE OF DEATH

"Oh God, lead us from the unreal to the real...From death to immortality."

—Hindu Peace Prayer

What if the cancer had killed me? On my deathbed, would I still rhapsodize about the infinite capacity for good in everything? Maybe once I reached the other side of the veil, but here on earth, death can be disconcerting. Many of us wonder about death. *Why do we need both life and death? Why do our loved ones have to die? Couldn't we all just live forever?*

If this chapter was a sermon, I would start by offering the congregation a multiple-choice quiz.

Question: What is the purpose of death?
   a. Death scares the crap out of us and makes us completely dysfunctional.
   b. Death amplifies the precious nature of life.
   c. Death teaches us there is no death.
   d. Death leads us from the unreal to the real.
   e. All of the above.

I'm going with e. All of the above.

a. Death scares the crap out of us and makes us completely dysfunctional:

Many smarter-than-me people believe the awareness of death underpins all of our actions. There are many dysfunctional manifestations related to death anxiety. Some people engage in risky behavior. Oddly, they attempt to stave off death by courting death. Others hold still so death won't find them. These people are afraid to live before they die.

That was me. When my mother was diagnosed with cancer, I stayed close to home to try and spackle the status quo. If I could just be still, hold my breath, and hold everything in place, maybe everything would be alright. Maybe my mother wouldn't die, and my world would remain intact.

My mother did die and afterwards, it took me a long time to let go of the "standing still." I used excessive caution in many early life choices. This gave me an illusion of control, but really all it did was contribute to a stifled life and an inner sense of "quiet desperation."[19]

b. Death makes life precious:

Our Town, a mystical play by Thornton Wilder, illuminates life's preciousness. One of the characters, Emily, dies at the age of 26. She rests in the graveyard with other characters that have died. There, she asks the stage manager (God) if she can go back to her life for one more day. The other dead folks advise against it. Then the stage manager reluctantly grants her wish.

Emily returns home on her 12th birthday. The people in her family bustle about, getting ready for the day. They take each other for granted and fail to recognize the immensity of the small

---

[19] Henry David Thoreau: "The mass of men lead lives of quiet desperation."

moments embedded in an ordinary morning. Emily becomes overwhelmed with the fragile, fleeting beauty of it all and says:

It goes so fast. We don't have time to look at one another. (She breaks down sobbing; she looks around) I didn't realize. All that was going on in life and we never noticed. Take me back—up the hill—to my grave. But first: Wait! One more look. Good-by, Good-by, world. Good-by, Grover's Corners. Mama and Papa. Good-by to clocks ticking. And Mama's sunflowers. And food and coffee. And new-ironed dresses and hot baths; and sleeping and waking up. Oh, earth, you're too wonderful for anybody to realize you. (She asks abruptly through her tears) Do any human beings ever realize life while they live it?—every, every minute?

The stage manager replies, "Saints and poets maybe. They do some."[iii]

Death is our opportunity to live like the saints and poets. We must realize the precious nature of life while we live it. We must live before we die.

c. Death teaches us there is no death:

I've been death adjacent on many occasions. I worked as a nurse in major medical centers where I tended to the sickest of the sick. Family members, friends, and pets have died. In ministry, I've blessed dead bodies and learned how to put the fun in funerals.

Despite all this exposure to death, at times I feel like Woody Allen, who said, "I'm not afraid of death, I just don't want to be there when it happens." When I got cancer, yes, I had beautiful moments of witnessing the precious nature of life. I learned to "bear the beams of love" that others bestowed upon me when they thought I might die.[20] In many ways, the experience was touching and glorious, but I still didn't feel ready to go.

---

20 Excerpt from *The Little Black Boy*, a poem by William Blake: "and we are put on earth a little space, that we may learn to bear the beams of love."

I wondered, *How can death happen to me? Others can die, I've seen it. But I cannot imagine not being here, as me.*

I've facilitated more than 100 memorials. I serve people of all religions and no religion. With each memorial, I do my best to speak as honestly as possible while honoring the beliefs of the deceased. No matter what the belief—whether it's religion, or no religion, or science—each time I come to the same conclusion. We do not die. We transform.

The compost cycle provides an amazing demonstration of eternal life through transformation. Food scraps and decomposing plants meet in the mystery to create something unfathomable. The miracle of chemistry creates life-giving soil that will someday grow plants. The plants mature to nourish other living things. These living things poop, die, and decompose—and the cycle goes on and on into perpetuity.

Some people don't like being compared to compost, but it's such an accessible example of the nature of infinite being. The compost cycle teaches us death is inconceivable. The part of us that thinks "death won't happen to me" is correct. We are immortal beings. Our current life is a "parenthesis in eternity."[iv] Even in the face of an inevitable expiration date, we must live like the truth of eternity is true. Because eternity *is* true.

d. Death leads us from the unreal to the real:

Death *seems* real, in that heartbeats, breath, and brain activities will one day cease for all of us. But death is *unreal*, because a larger, all-encompassing reality continues beyond the termination of the body. Our *awareness* of death can help us discern the unreal from the real. Death helps us reimagine priorities. It helps us discover the "realness" of that which matters most.

While we're here on earth, we chase the unreal. The ego tells us our lives are meaning-full only if we attain certain achievements—so we pursue meaning-less props. We chase after control, material accessories, approval, addictions, and accolades. This endless chasing can be another futile strategy to ward off the perceived emptiness of inevitable death.

But Emily's speech in *Our Town* speaks of coffee, and sleeping, and sunflowers. Simple, everyday things. Emily recognized the small details of her life as an endless parade of blessings infused with grace. That's true for all of us. Everything is God-infused, and the God infusion is real. As we focus on this truth, we move from the unreal to the real. We renounce *attachment* to things that do not matter; things that cannot save us from death. Our renunciation invites us to cherish life and death as a continuum of transient, yet eternal blessings. Forms change; blessedness remains the same—an ever-constant reality in the bliss of immortal mortal existence.

A beloved practitioner, Fred, who laughed at my "inconsolable whiner" prayer request, passed away recently. I told this story at his memorial:

When I started at the church, Fred often told me, "Reverend Bonnie, I'm praying for your gumption." It was a good prayer, because I needed fortitude in the beginning of my ministry. When I settled down and became more skilled and peaceful, Fred began telling me a new story. Every now and then he took me aside and said, "Reverend Bonnie, I'm afraid you're going to leave us. What if you get a better job offer? What if you hit the big time?"

I always smiled and said, "Well, Fred, what if *this* is the big time? What if Ventura is big enough for God? What if this is where I'm supposed to be?" My one regret in these conversations with Fred is that I didn't add, "Fred, this is the big time—because *you're* here, and because people like you are here, and your lives matter."

It's true. Because we are here, we have meaning. We all matter to God. It couldn't be any other way. The small is real. The mundane is sacred and meaningful. Beauty is the big time. You are real, sacred, and meaningful. I know if I were to memorialize you someday, I could totally put the fun in your funeral. I would celebrate what's real about you. I would cherish the beauty in the tiny transient details of your life. Then I would affirm how the energy of "realness" never dies. It is here before, during, and after we inhabit these mortal bodies.

You are the big time. We are the big time. And the small, shifting details of our sweet lives are beautiful, now and forever. That's what's real. But let's not wait until our funerals to figure that out.

Reflections

Head: What are you waiting for? How might you live before you die?

Heart: Divine Love, teach me to live in the freedom of infinite immortality.

Hands: Go out and live before you die. Do something you've always wanted to do.

PART FOUR:

PRICELESS

FROM GRASPING TO GRACE

> *"You are in a state of grace in which you know you are connected to God and thus free from the effects of anyone or anything external to yourself."*
>
> —Dr. Wayne Dyer

COVID caused many of us to face impermanence and mortality. Our church shut down during the pandemic and switched to online virtual services. As we started the reopening process, we saw COVID had impacted our church. Attendance and donations dropped significantly, and we worried about sustainability. Our faith told us this was an opportunity for reinvention. Our fear told us to be concerned. So one day, seven masked church leaders and I sat in a socially-distanced circle to discuss how we would address our situation.

I squirmed and proposed a costly social media marketing scheme.

"It seems risky given our current income," I said. "But maybe we should do it."

Our board president, Lonnie, is wise and wonderful. Therefore, I was not offended when she blurted, "You're prostituting yourself again, Bonnie."

"I'm not a prostitute, *you're* a prostitute," I blurted back, without knowing why.

Lonnie laughed and said, "You're just trying to fill the seats."

"But that's what ministers do." I whined. "We're supposed to grow our churches."

Lonnie emitted an eye roll heard 'round the world.

"There are prostitutes in the Bible," I said, clutching at straws.

We laughed again. Then Lonnie reminded me of a prior ministerial-prostitution-offense.

Our church is an historic building, often in need of renewal. Our basement room, used primarily for recovery-group meetings, was disgusting. The Palomino-toned paint was streaked and peeling. Shadows of aged coffee puddles stained the dirty pink carpet. Moisture seeped up from the ocean table below the foundation, creating crop circles around the coffee stains. The rug squished when we walked on it, and the room smelled like rancid socks. We affectionately referred to the whole scenario down there as "the swamp thing."

It was embarrassing. We respect our friends in recovery and wanted to provide them with a gracious space for healing. We needed about $50,000 to make that happen, but we didn't have that kind of money lying around. So my inner prostitute emerged.

I had a plan. I would verbally seduce a famous spiritual author to do an evening event at our church. We would charge attendees a lot of money, fill our large sanctuary, and raise all the funds needed for the repairs in one night.

I visualized huge checks pouring in. Then I put on my metaphorical thigh-high boots and a red leather bustier. I loitered beside an imaginary lamppost, like a strumpet, as I swiveled my hips, and all but hollered, "You want a date?" to every spiritual celebrity who would listen.

I had a few nibbles. I formed a connection with a super-famous author who was a household name. I won't reveal who it was. We'll just call him Dwayne. Dr. Dwayne Wire.

I had my people call Dwayne's people. By that, I mean I took a deep breath and dialed Dwayne's booking agent. Our church is a unique and appealing space with a large seating capacity and high visibility, so it might have been a tad enticing to him. Dwayne's people seemed interested. We were in serious negotiations, but when the question of fee came up, we couldn't pay what they required.

It was a very pleasant conversation. Dwayne's people were lovely and kind. We just weren't a good fit. I was disappointed, but realized disappointment isn't a reason to give up. Disappointment is an invitation to stay open. *Maybe I can think up new ways to prostitute myself!* I thought.

About those prostitutes in the Bible: Most normal ministers would go straight to your Whore of Babylon or Mary Magdalene (who probably wasn't really a prostitute).[21, 22] I believe some of your biggest biblical prostitutes were the money changers and merchants in the temple. These players employed earth-bound commerce strategies in a sacred space. They believed these actions were necessary for survival, personal gain, and God's approval.

For those of you unfamiliar with the Bible, Jesus and his disciples traveled to Jerusalem for Passover. They went to the temple and found people engaged in buying and selling wares.

---

21 The Whore of Babylon refers to a phrase in the book of Revelation, Chapter 17: "Mystery, Babylon the Great, the Mother of Prostitutes and Abominations of the Earth."

22 See *The Meaning of Mary Magdalene or The Wisdom Jesus*, both by Cynthia Bourgeault.

The merchants sold material goods, including animals for blood sacrifices. They did this because worshipers believed an animal sacrifice might impress God, as if to say, "Maybe God needs a little somethin' extra, so I can stay on 'His' good side." Some say when Jesus beheld the money changers, he got angry and drove them out. "My house will be a house of prayer, but you have made it a den of thieves," he said (Matthew 21:13).

Others deny Jesus was angry. We believe Jesus's actions implied a firm stand against bartering for God's blessings. Jesus refutes the consciousness that says, "God, if I offer this object to you, I hope you'll reward me." Jesus's actions challenge the mindset that begs, "If I spend some money on your behalf God, can you send a little good fortune my way?" Jesus *liberates* those of us who say, "God, I'll show you a dead chicken then *you* show me how much you care."

We all bargain with God from time to time, but this is unnecessary. While we're not liable to sacrifice a chicken on God's behalf, driving out the merchants represents the release of our attachment to a *transactional* relationship with the divine.[23] Jesus the Christ, the consciousness of oneness, encourages us to choose grace over grasping. He asks us to renounce bartering and instead, accept God's freely offered benevolence.

We do not need to buy God's love. The demonstration of God's love does not depend on sacrifice. God's love is complete and unconditional now. True, sometimes infinite love is invisible to us, but we make the infinite "real" to the extent we receive it. The only thing we sacrifice is our inability or unwillingness to partake of infinite love. The only condition of God's love is that it

---

23 For more information on this Biblical passage, see Mathew Fox's online meditation for April 1, 2021: *Eckhart on Driving Merchants from our Souls and Temples - Daily Meditations with Matthew Fox.*

must be received. We receive God's love by accepting it—and by giving it away.

I was immersed in transactional consciousness when I charged after spiritual celebrities, wearing my metaphorical thigh-high stilettos, begging, "Please fix our church. If you say yes, we'll show you a good time. Then *you* can show us the money."

This was me clinging to known, rational material resources as the *only* solution to a challenging situation. Material resources may be helpful. There's nothing wrong with matter. But sometimes our dependency on matter obscures a spiritual solution. Sometimes the one who sees the bigger picture has an amazing plan, and if we're patient, divine beneficence will emerge to reveal her holy flowchart.

Several weeks after Dwayne said no, I got an unexpected email from a rarely seen church member. It was a transcript of a University of Pennsylvania commencement speech by a young man named Nipun Mehta. Nipun spoke at this Ivy League graduation because he and some friends founded an organization called ServiceSpace.[24] This organization spreads goodness all over the world. Among other things, they leverage technology to create a culture of compassion, generosity, and kindness.

Nipun's graduation speech was about a pilgrimage across India. He and his wife, Guri, walked 600 miles with no amenities and no money. They went on this journey to serve, to relinquish attachments, and to grow strong in the grace of intangible spiritual gifts.

Nipun ended his speech with a story about his great-grandfather in India—a man of little wealth who walked every day. As he walked, he fed the anthills he encountered with small pinches of wheat flower. This was a tiny act of kindness many

---

24 For more information on ServiceSpace go to www.servicespace.org.

would call meaningless. But the consciousness of this gentle soul who offered kindness to ants— "the least of our brothers and sisters" (Matthew 25:40)—shaped the consciousness of Nipun's ancestors. This ant-feeding consciousness shaped Nipun, a man whose organization now inspires radical kindness in millions of beings around the world.

Nipun wrote, *"Today those ants and the ant hills are gone, but my great grandpa's spirit is very much embedded in all my actions and their future ripples. It is precisely these small, often invisible, acts of inner transformation that mold the stuff of our being, and bend the arc of our shared destiny. On your walk, today and always, I wish you the eyes to see the anthills and the heart to feed them with joy. May you be blessed. Change yourself—change the world."*[25]

Reflections

***Head**: Have you ever bargained or engaged in other transactions with the divine?*

***Heart**: Divine Love, help me partake of your free and unconditional grace. Help me give and receive the bounty of creation that exists all around me.*

***Hands**: Practice flourishing. Discover some new ways to give and receive without attachment to results.*

---

[25] For the full Nipun Mehta U-Penn graduation speech, go to *Paths Are Made By Walking*, by Nipun Mehta (www.dailygood.org).

KINDNESS

"No act of kindness, no matter how small, is ever wasted."
—Aesop

He had me at "ants." I emailed Nipun and asked if he would do a speaker event for us. Nipun gets requests to speak at venues around the world, but he said yes to our modest center in Ventura. When I asked about his fee, he said, "I don't have one." His agenda was to go where the universe led him, to share his message of kindness, and to sow seeds of goodness that would inevitably ripple outward to create more goodness.

Nipun—a tall Indian man with boyish charm and a warm smile—arrived at our church. He wore a plain navy-blue button-down shirt and khakis that were a little frayed at the hem. He was enthusiastic about everything. He all but bounced when he complimented us on the music we provided for the event, the hotel accommodations, and the roominess of my Honda Element.

During the evening event, he spoke about his walk across India—the hardships, the joy, the growth. The attendees were mesmerized by the message and the messenger.

Afterwards, he held a question-and-answer session that went something like this:

"I'm having trouble with my teenage son, what should I do?" Sandy asked.

"I would suggest you practice small acts of kindness," Nipun replied.

"I've been unemployed for six months," George said. "I'm desperate. Can you help?"

"Yes, performing small acts of kindness will open your heart and take your mind off your troubles," Nipun advised. "Eventually, you'll be changed from the inside out and something wonderful will find you."

"I'm concerned about violence in the world," Ellen said. "How can someone like me make a difference?"

"Focus on small acts of kindness and trust the ripples," Nipun recommended.

There was a long pause as people contemplated the questions and the answers. Then Nipun asked, "Who else has a question so I can suggest small acts of kindness?"

The audience laughed and appeared to wonder, *Do small acts really make a difference? Does kindness offer an answer to all of life's questions? Can dedicating ourselves to meticulous kindness change the world?*

We didn't know the answers to these questions—but Nipun and his work started us on a gentle path of exploration.

Reflections

Head: What do you believe about the power of small acts of kindness?

Heart: Divine Love, give me the faith to bless my world with small acts of kindness.

Hands: Perform an act of goodness as "small" as feeding the anthills of the world. Repeat.

Nipun Mehta

23

INVISIBLE AND INVINCIBLE

"Only your compassion and your loving kindness are invincible, and without limit."

—Thich Nhat Hanh

Small acts of kindness change the world, yet it is difficult for the ego to understand this. It takes a while for the linear logic of the separate-self-illusion, to catch up with the mystery of unlimited love. Fortunately, God helps us make the leap from logic to love, with tangible evidence of small yet mighty things.

Small is powerful. A gnat flies up your nose and ruins your meditation. A flea disrupts a dog's nap. An infant—a six-pound prune of a being—can rattle an entire household with screaming, poop, and mega-cuteness. The power of smallness exists everywhere.

One day a few years ago, I put on my rubber boots and stepped into our back yard to rake out our aviary. We have a large, enclosed space where we keep cockatiels, guinea pigs, a 20-pound bunny rabbit, and two box turtles.

Our box turtles, Carolina and Duke, are ancient—but they still get sexy with each other. Yes, there is turtle-porn in my backyard. It's not exciting to watch—it's a little slow—but evidently still effective because one day, I found a baby turtle languishing on the dirt floor of the aviary. He was no bigger than a quarter. I couldn't get him to eat or crawl, so I picked him up, stuck him in the pocket of my pink hoodie, and hauled him off to the vet.

I checked in with the receptionist.

"What's your pet's name?"

"Let's call him Baby Turtle," I replied.

"I'm assuming it's a turtle?" the receptionist said.

"That's right."

"How much does Baby Turtle weigh?" she asked.

"I'm not sure if you understand what we're dealin' with here," I said. I pulled Baby Turtle out of my jacket pocket, placed his quarter-sized self in the palm of my hand, and showed him to the receptionist.

She broke into a huge smile. "On My Goodness! Jessica! Diana! Jenn! Get out here! We've got us a tiny turtle at reception."

The vet techs came out of the back offices and gathered around the flat brown disk in my palm. The clients in the waiting area left their cat carriers to come and see. Some pulled their reluctant dogs over, all to marvel at this powerful messenger. Baby Turtle became an instant celebrity. People snapped photographs and peppered me with questions. His smallness was a magnet.

Eventually we pushed through the paparazzi and made our way to the vet's exam room for the turtle's little physical. It turned out he was fine. Jenn, one of the admiring vet techs, fell in love with Baby Turtle. She had a terrarium set-up at home with lights and plants, so I said she could keep him. Jenn re-named him Squirt. She placed him in his new home with all the required accoutrements.

Later, the story of Squirt wound up in a Sunday sermon. That Sunday I said, "Squirt was a gift from God, sent to the aviary in my back yard to give us a message…a message about what, you might ask?"

"Let's start by putting the baby turtle in perspective," I continued. "Consider the ratio. Squirt is to the vet clinic as you or I are to the galaxy. He is tiny in the scheme of things. Practically invisible. And yet Squirt was a super-hero. He brought goodwill to many people. I'm sure those who met Squirt that day went home and talked to their families and friends about the tiny turtle. That small Squirt rippled, brothers and sisters…"

I thought I heard an "Amen," and then a "Hallelujah."

I went on: "Squirt is a lesson for all of us on how little things can inspire great love. How someone even as small as you or me can create a wave of goodwill in the galaxy."

Then I asked the congregation, "Will you believe with me that small, good things have unlimited power? Will you trust that just as Squirt had an impact, we can positively influence the lives of many? If you believe, will you start some tiny waves of goodness today? Please join me in doing so. Send your invincible kindness out into the universe. Then trust your small kindness makes a big difference. And if you ever succumb to doubt, remember our master teacher, small in size, but big in spirit. Our brother Squirt—who became a tsunami of goodwill. Let us pray!"

Reflections

Head: What small acts of kindness have made a big difference in your life?

Heart: Divine Love, help me offer invisible, invincible kindness to myself and others.

Hands: Have a conversation with someone about the power of the small. Listen diligently, knowing this in itself is an act of kindness.

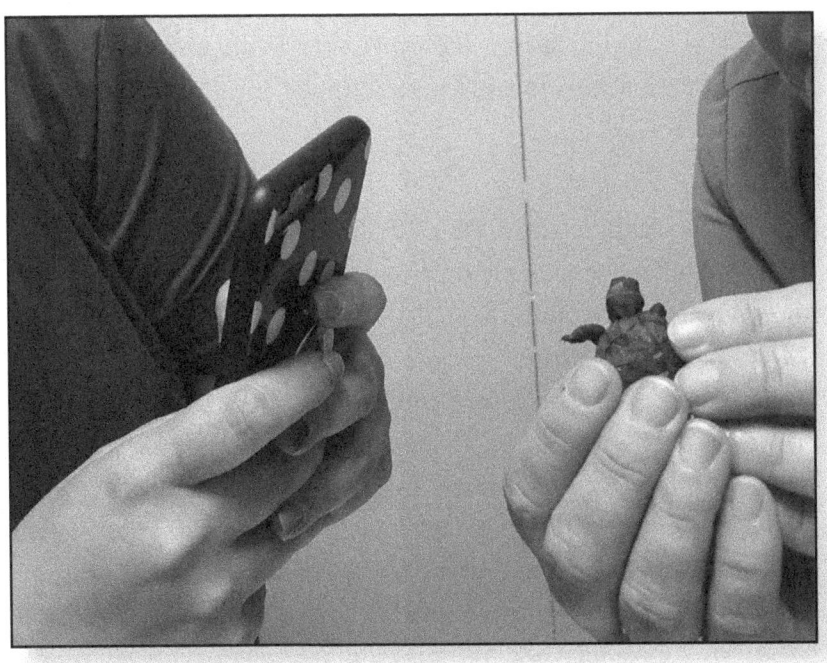

Baby Turtle (Squirt) during his physical exam.

THE ADVANCES OF LOVE

"I alone cannot change the world, but I can cast a stone across the waters to create many ripples."
—Mother Teresa

Nipun's small-act-of-kindness path brought him to the Obama White House to serve on a panel that addressed policy regulations on poverty and inequality in America. He posted this on the ServiceSpace website:

"*At our first White House meeting, we did an introductory circle on the question—what gives you hope? Before I could think up something smart to say, :) it was already my turn to speak. And this is what spontaneously came to my mind, 'Well, what gives me hope is love. What gives me hope is reading the NY Times story of how one person paid for coffee for the person behind her in line, and two hundred and twenty-six people followed suit. Two hundred and twenty-six people were voluntarily moved to pay it forward. What gives me hope is that life unfailingly responds to the advances of love.'*"[26]

How wonderful that someone sat in the White House and talked about "the advances of love." I wondered if our church would ever have such an impact.

---

26 Nipun Mehta, web reference: https://nipun.servicespace.org/docs/Obama).

"These things ye shall do and more" is a paraphrase of the words of Jesus in John 14:12. I used to take this phrase literally, thinking that someday, like Jesus, we would be able to raise the dead and heal the sick. I remember a prominent metaphysical teacher once saying she was "practicing on dead birds."

Maybe we will raise the dead and heal the sick literally, but all things start in consciousness. Meaning, we begin to heal the sick and raise the dead in a mystical sense. We address the *illusions* of deadness and sickness held inside by so many of us. We heal deadness of spirit and sickness of the soul.

The pandemic exacerbated many of our sick-and-dead tendencies. People fought over masks, vaccines, inequity, money, and politics. The world felt enraged and outraged. It still does. Our collective anger is like another mask, a façade to cover our uncertainty, our loss of control, and our hopelessness. Anger is a symptom of fear; and fear is a symptom of ignorance. We are ignorant to the true nature of being. We forget about heaven on earth. We forget our holy connection with God and the entire cosmos. Evidence of our forgetfulness is everywhere.

Our forgetfulness is spread upon the 24-hour news cycle, in the parade of screaming headlines. Forgetfulness also shows up in our individual lives and how we relate to each other. On another trip to the vet's office during COVID, I saw signage begging clients to be kind with the words: "The whole world is struggling. Please be kind to the people who show up to help." Then I saw a sign at the DMV—the DMV which is often the butt of jokes about inefficiency and grumpiness. "Stand in Line and Please Be Kind," it read.

Our city performed road repairs near the start of the pandemic shutdown. Our street was torn up for several months and this made going out, getting home, and parking inconvenient. Every time I approached a member of the construction team to ask a question, I felt them brace for criticism. I spoke to a friend who works in construction and asked, "Why do the people working on our road seem like they're afraid of me?"

"Because most people only approach them to yell at them," she replied.

Another time long before the pandemic, one of our congregants, influenced by Nipun's work sent a thank you note with some coffee and cookies to our local public works department. The public works manager called him back and started to cry on the phone. He said it was the first time in 20-plus years of service that anyone offered his department support or praise.

Again, I think of the teachings of Jesus, raising the dead and healing the sick. If we're kind to vet techs, DMV employees, road construction teams, and the people who administer our water supply, doesn't this kindness raise and heal all of us? Kindness helps us remember who we are—one with God and one with the cosmos. And when we remember who we are, we are kind. Kindness and remembrance go together like a chicken and an egg. One leads to the other, and no one knows which comes first.

There may be evidence of our self-forgetfulness in the world. We may mire ourselves in that alleged evidence. But if we look closely, we also see signs of our true, benevolent nature. Kindness prevails in the darkest circumstances. At any moment, we can choose to behold evidence of goodness, then amplify that goodness with more goodness. We practice kindness at the vet's and the DMV. We praise road construction teams and bring them Christmas and Hanukkah candy. We celebrate those who silently serve us in so many ways. We invoke kindness in all the tiny moments in our individual yet shared lives, to magnify our ultimate interconnection.

I believe this is what Jesus meant when he said, "These things, you shall do and more." Love gives each of us unique gifts and circumstances. We are called to use these gifts in the small opportunities that beckon to us. Rumi said, "There are hundreds of ways to kneel and kiss the ground." There are infinite ways to raise the dead and heal the sick through personal acts of kindness. We serve the divine in all things and dead eyes come alive again. Heartsickness heals. Hope becomes greater than hatred. We move from *beholding* kindness to *becoming* kindness. And we are privileged—absolutely honored—to be noble participants in life's magnanimous response to the advances of love.

Reflections

Head: What deadness would you like to raise? What sickness needs to be healed?

Heart: Divine Love, help me to behold and become kindness everywhere.

Hands: Do one small act of kindness and make up a grand story about the potential ripples. Also notice how the act of kindness changes you – because kindness ripples inwardly as well as outwardly.

25

PRICELESS

"The kingdom of heaven is like a merchant seeking beautiful pearls, who, when he had found one pearl of great price, went and sold all that he had and bought it."

—Jesus

Our church has maintained a relationship with Nipun and ServiceSpace for many years. The blessings continue to flow. Through ServiceSpace, we've met humanitarian leaders from all over the world. Several of us encountered Sister Lucy, a remarkable Catholic nun who works with underserved women and children in India.[27] Through faith and persistence, she gathered food from local merchants to feed thousands of people when her city's food supply was cut off during the pandemic. A disciple from the Gandhi lineage, Arun Bhatt, came and spoke at our church. He taught us to say "Jai Sri Krishna" in moments of vexation with difficult people.[28] On a ZOOM call, we met Lily Yeh, a Korean woman who creates art out of broken glass and bones.[29] She works

---

27 Sister Lucy Kurien, www.servicespace.org/blog/view.php?id=26254.
28 Jai Sri Krishna (pronounced Jay Shree Krishna) is a Hindu phrase meaning "victory to Krishna." Krishna is often seen as a symbol of love so a translation of the phrase could be "victory to love."
29 For more information on the work of Lily Yeh, go to www.barefootartists.org.

with shattered communities to build mosaics and monuments to the living and the dead.

Many famous authors and luminaries participate in ServiceSpace. Yet, the organization does not value famous or enlightened people more than us regular folks. They believe everyone can serve. Everyone can remember our divine connection through acts of kindness.

Over the years, I've asked Nipun, "How do you do it? How do you continue to build this amazing organization?" He explains their design principles. They trust in the innate goodness of humanity. They focus on depth rather than breadth. They give everything away for free. They don't advertise or fundraise. They have no paid staff; rather, they enlist thousands of volunteers in selfless service.

ServiceSpace employs practices that are counter-intuitive to modern business and non-profit minds, yet their embrace is wide. They welcome 20,000 visitors to their websites every hour of every day. They distribute 70 million emails per year. Meditation gatherings called Awakin' circles thrive in more than 100 cities around the world.

As the conversation with Nipun continues, I ask him to explain the deeper subtleties of ServiceSpace. He talks, and I listen. Eventually, he'll pause to take a breath and I say, "I have no idea what you're talking about, but I know it's good and I want to understand better."

Then one day, I got it. I understood just a little more of the ServiceSpace mystique. Nipun copied me on an email he wrote to a global organization that had expressed an interest in partnering with ServiceSpace. They had lots of questions and Nipun responded.

I read Nipun's answers to their questions, none of which fit into "normal" organizational boxes. Then the heavens opened.

God metaphorically stretched a long hairy arm out of the heavens and gave me a post-it. The post-it said, "Treasures in heaven."

From the Bible: "Do not store up for yourselves treasures on earth, where moths and rust destroy, and where thieves break in and steal. But store up for yourselves treasures in heaven, where moths and rust do not destroy, and where thieves do not break in and steal. For where your treasure is, there your heart will be also" (Matthew 6:19-21).

What does this mean in terms of running a business, a non-profit, or a life?

Storing treasures on earth represents dependency on material things. Storing treasures in heaven refers to investing in divine consciousness. This Bible verse tells us to identify that which is truly valuable and invest our energy there. We remain unattached to outcome and refrain from over-valuing material results. There is no need to chase success based on the typical barometers of worthiness such as "likes" on social media, money, and influence. There is no need to invest in impermanent things, for these things will become dust. Moths and rust will destroy them. Instead we invest our energy in eternal values that endure beneath all surface changes. We do so with rigorous attention and intention. Kindness, grace, generosity, compassion, love, joy, peace, our soul's purpose—all of these things are steadfast, infinite, and expansive. These are our treasures in heaven.

Rumi expressed this same concept when he wrote, "If it is bread that you seek, you will have bread. If it is the soul you seek, you will find the soul. If you understand this secret, you know you are that which you seek." Meaning if we seek matter, we'll have matter. If we seek soul, we'll have soul. If we understand the relationship between matter and soul; if we recognize matter is a lovely yet impermanent part of creation and soul is eternal grace; then we anchor in the truth of the I Am that already is.

We become aware of our existence in the one, as the one. This is priceless.

Priceless is not cheap—it is pure. When we engage with the priceless we receive spiritual riches beyond definition. We embody the capacity to move through life in oneness as love. The values we cherish become form and we express the pearl of great price. "The kingdom of heaven is like a merchant seeking beautiful pearls, who, when he had found one pearl of great price, went and sold all that he had and bought it" (Matthew 13: 45-46).

Who or what is the "pearl of great price?" Is it Jesus? Buddha? Nipun? Is it me? Is it you? Is it God? The answer is yes—and so much more. The pearl of great price is divine consciousness, union with source, and the willingness to rest in that which brings forth our true nature. It is the unspeakable joy that informs all of creation, the kingdom of heaven spread upon the earth. The pearl of great price is meant to be shared, for sharing reveals the interconnection of the cosmos. Through sharing, we become the union we seek.

Is this hard to believe? Difficult to imagine, or understand? Do you need proof these ideas are real?

I know I often waver in the face of obstacles. I sometimes still believe choosing radical trust in eternal values over material gain will ruin everything. I know the Bible verse well, where Jesus instructs us to "seek first the kingdom of God, then all you need will be added unto you" (Matthew 6:33). It sounds like a good plan—but I still crave proof of security. According to Lonnie, I still occasionally act like a big prostitute. But then I think about all we've gained through our priceless relationship with ServiceSpace—all of the intangibles I've described—and then one more *material* demonstration, a demonstration that offered us pricelessness plus proof.

Our relationship with ServiceSpace started with "the swamp

thing" room. We began a well-intentioned journey to create a welcoming space. First we clutched at a spiritual celebrity because we thought he would bring us material wealth. We grasped at that which moth and rust would destroy. When it turned out the celebrity was too expensive, we said no. Then the priceless emerged. Unbeknownst to us at the time, we placed our treasure in heaven.

Nipun was literally priceless. He didn't charge us a fee. More importantly, he was spiritually priceless in that he offered us things Dr. Dwayne could never give us. Dr. Dwayne would have provided us with a great event and then he would have moved on. Nipun gave us a great event and planted seeds that multiplied. We formed an enduring relationship. We grew together in the exploration of radical spiritual principles. We moved past a sense of futility as we learned to engage in small acts of kindness. These actions changed our community and the world around us. Meeting Nipun was like winning the lottery—a priceless lottery where love was the jackpot.

We remained true to our values, we put our treasure in heaven, we found Nipun, and soon the things we needed for "the swamp thing" renovation flowed to us. The money came in through many small, generous donations. Volunteers and professionals became friends as they transformed the swampy room into a welcoming haven for people in recovery. We eliminated the squishy rug and installed tiles to keep the underlying ocean table at bay. We decorated the room with donated furniture and throw rugs. We set up a spiritual library to provide free books to anyone who is interested. The heart of the space expanded to include veterans, meditators, a local children's theater group, and other seekers. Today, lives change in that sacred room and the changed lives change even more lives—generations of lives.

The process of renovation—of a room, a church, a life, or a

planet—is often different than what we expect. When we get our matter-obsessed attachment out of the way, we allow a mystical vision to enter the equation. Mystical grace assembles seemingly random pieces to create an infinite outcome. How glorious it is to trust in the power of the priceless—the treasures that matter most. How glorious it is to allow the pearl of great price to make our lives luminous from within.

Reflections:

Head: Is there any place in your life where you over-invest in that which moth and rust will destroy (impermanence)?

Heart: Divine Love, guide me to invest in precious and priceless values. Guide me to invest in my soul's purpose.

Hands: Choose a priceless value and take one small but bold action to express it in the world. Notice what comes up for you as you invest in "treasures in heaven."

PART FIVE:

DANCING IN THE UNCONDITIONAL ABSOLUTE

LICKING THE LAW OF ATTRACTION

"Acting silly is one of the primal pleasures."
—Marty Rubin

"I want to write a little book." I said this to my friend, Alice, who is a healer and body worker.

"What's it about?" she asked.

"I don't know. A bunch of spiritual essays, but weird. Like me. Unconventional spirituality. There may be some cursing. Plus there's a Law of Attraction story about a time I wanted to lick our veterinarian."

"Aren't you married?" Alice said.

"Oh, no, not like that. I didn't want to lick the vet in a sexy way. It's, you know, like David Sedaris," I said, referring to the great essayist.

"David Sedaris licked his veterinarian?"

I laughed, "No, not his vet. But he licked a ton of other stuff. He wrote an essay, *A Plague of Tics*, about how when he was a kid, he used to lick mailboxes and light switches.[v] Because they were there, and he had to. It was a compulsion. Same as me and the vet."

Alice nodded as if she understood completely. Like I said, she's a healer.

There are many people in my spiritual circles who swear by The Law of Attraction. If you want to change your life, you change your thinking. *The Secret*, a book and movie that was released in 2006, put the Law of Attraction on the map. Millions of people learned about the power of manifestation at that time. We did our best to use cause and effect, or Law of Attraction principles, to control our thoughts and create desired results.

One day, *The Secret* followed me into the vet's office to lead me beside unstill waters, namely a river of drool. It started with a benign thought: *Bonnie, wouldn't it be funny if you licked the veterinarian and blamed one of the dogs?*

It made sense, sort of. The vet and I frequently have to co-wrestle an unwilling animal into submission. Animal wrestling is a full-contact, high-anxiety sport, and my dogs are fear lickers. Somehow it seemed like it would be fun to throw my own tongue into the mix. *Why not?* I thought. *People fart and blame the dog all the time.* The power of my thoughts told me, *lick the vet, for the sake of comedy…see if you can get away with it.*

All licking aside, I appreciate our vet. He is skilled and reasonable, not prone to order thousands of dollars' worth of intrusive medical tests for a lump or a vomit. He seems genuinely interested in the things that fascinate me—Bartie's toxic anal glands, the oozing pustule on our guinea pig's nipple, or what to do when your dog eats the rumen of a dead cow.

Now none of that should inspire licking, but once I had the thought, it latched onto me like a tic. It stuck in my brain and festered. Every time I entered the vet's office with *any* of our animals, *The Secret* whispered in my ear: "You attract what you think about!" "When you believe it, you will achieve it!" "When you see it, you will be it." This scared me and made me try and *stop* thinking about licking the vet. Trying to stop made me think about licking the vet even harder.

One day, our cat, Audrey, went in for an eye infection. I met the doctor in his examination room where he switched off the lights and whipped out his manly ophthalmoscope to examine Audrey's eye. We were in the dark, restraining a squirming cat who was eager to slink back into her carrier. I thought about her rough cat's tongue. The vet's head bent toward me, and I felt my tongue inch toward his ear. Then his assistant turned on the lights and I backed off.

The vet sent us home with eye-drops. *All finished*, I thought.

But a few months later, my tongue rallied. Our dogs, Stella and Bartie, needed a vet-check. Our vet is kind and gentle; however, he inspires terror in the dogs. They stampede around the tiny exam room like the wild ponies of Chincoteague. They can't escape, so they shrink under his wooden bench. "*Maybe he won't see us here,*" they seem to think. When that doesn't work, they claw at the walls in a Shawshank attempt to tunnel out.[30]

The vet needed to lance a boil on Stella's neck. Even though the urge to lick the vet is not sexual, this scene was like an operatic bacchanal. There was yelping, groping, and writhing under the fluorescent lights on the pale-yellow linoleum floor. The vet cornered Stella between the door and the wooden bench. I flung myself on top of the pile to hold Stella down. Bartie leapt in to save his sister, so there were four of us, an undulating tangle of limbs, torsos, tongues, and tails—plus a large needle headed for that boil.

The vet leaned in to do the procedure. His neck was

---

30   Refers to *The Shawshank Redemption,* a 1994 movie based on a book by Stephen King. I don't want to give away the ending…but there is an escape from prison that may or may not involve a tunnel.

strategically placed, directly under my tongue. So again, I thought, *Lick him.*

Abruptly, he pulled away. "Whoa…" he said. "I think we could do with one less *tongue* in the room."

I froze. *Holy Mother of God*, I said to myself. *Was it me? Did the power of my thoughts create a reality? Did my tongue just do The Secret?*

Reflections:

Head: What has been your experience with the Law of Attraction?

Heart: Divine Love, teach me to celebrate the strange business of being human.

Hands: Model self-acceptance. Find someone you trust and tell them a funny story about one of your quirks.

27

THE HOLY GOAT

Out beyond ideas of wrong-doing and right-doing, there is a field. I'll meet you there. When the soul lies down in that grass, the world is too full to talk about."

—Rumi

My experience at the vet's office, among other things, led me to deeper consideration of the nature of reality. I began to ponder what we might call absolute or unconditional reality.

Absolute reality is placeless, spaceless, and timeless. It lives here and now, yet beyond our typical understanding of this realm of existence. Mystics may refer to absolute reality as the kingdom of heaven. Others call it wholeness—a wholeness so vast it includes the appearance of brokenness. Absolute reality exists beyond relative perspectives. It is Rumi's field "out beyond ideas of wrong-doing and right-doing." It is a place that includes the mystery of licking or not licking a veterinarian. It is a soul-infused space where "the world is too full to talk about."

I've read about absolute reality in the writing of great teachers: Mother Teresa, who says, "We are a drop in the ocean;" and Rumi, who says, "We are the entire ocean in a drop." I've read Jeff Foster, who says absolute reality is like the ocean and we are like waves arising out of an eternal sea. I've studied Rupert Spira, who refers to absolute reality as awareness, or consciousness, or our awareness of being aware.

All of these intellectual ideas about absolute reality are lovely, but our thinking minds can't always grasp ineffable concepts. Again, it's the difference between reading a book about swimming and getting into the water. We need to experience absolute reality to deepen our knowing of it. Therefore, my greatest teacher of absolute reality was a goat. Blondie, the holy goat.

I lived in Manhattan in my late 20s. My apartment was on the upper west side. I went to the opera frequently. I saw plays, visited museums, enjoyed great food, and shopped. Every cultural, culinary, and mercantile advantage was there for me.

When I was called to our church, Hugh and I moved to Santa Paula, California. Santa Paula is a small, charming, western town. I like the cowboy feel of the place. There's a great feed store and occasionally a horse ambles through the citrus groves nearby. But it's not Manhattan. There is no opera. *There is no opera in Santa Paula, therefore Santa Paula is too small.* This became my mantra and my reality. Then, my husband and I rescued a goat.

Each Christmas Eve, we perform a church play. Whatever the play, it's always a thinly veiled excuse for a farm animal finale. We invite a goat, a donkey, a pig, a miniature horse, a sheep, a turkey, or whoever our handler, Tina, can wrangle into our sanctuary. The choir sings a triumphal song while the animals stroll in, honking, whinnying, and sometimes refusing to move. Poop often makes an appearance. Eventually everyone makes it to the stage for a stunning tableau. We light candles and sing *Silent Night*. Sometimes the animals join in, to amplify the song of praise for all beings.

One year we were short a goat. We learned of a petting zoo about to "retire" a goat, and by "retire" I mean they were going to turn her into a tamale. My husband and I swooped in and rescued

Blondie, a big skinny, affectionate girl. We gave the petting zoo people some cash and escorted Blondie into the back of my SUV.

We took her to our home in Santa Paula. There she head-butted our dogs and bleated her objections every time we abandoned her in the backyard. She found comfort in eating weeds. Her comfort food evolved into a case of explosive diarrhea. It happens.

But when Christmas Eve arrived, Blondie held it together. She stood proudly onstage with the rest of the Christmas animals. There she devoured a few paper ornaments from the Christmas tree. Afterwards, she enjoyed meeting the congregation. Then she returned to our home to await future placement on a goat-friendly farm.

Often when performers experience a meteoric rise to stardom, they struggle with the pressure. You've seen the tabloids. Nouveaux celebrities who hit the spotlight in a hurry may drink, carouse, and engage in other rambunctious behaviors. This was Blondie. Two days after her Christmas Eve debut, Blondie decided to paint the town. She butted a hole in our rickety wooden fence and embarked on a wild romp through the streets of Santa Paula.

I saw the goat-sized hole in the fence and panicked. How could I be so careless as to lose an entire goat?

"Hugh!" I yelled. "Blondie's gone!"

We assembled some make-shift goat seeking paraphernalia (mostly carrots) and wandered the streets of our town bleating, "Blondie…Blondie…" In that moment, I understood the nature of absolute reality with exquisite clarity.

Santa Paula was once too tiny to tolerate. Now, from the perspective of a goat gone wild, it was immense. There were hundreds of tasty backyards where Blondie could graze. I thought, *I'll never find her.* The rogue goat was a mere speck in the vastness of Santa Paula.

The size of Santa Paula flipped on me. I was absolutely sure

Santa Paula was too small, but the relative size of Santa Paula depended on context generated by *me*. The size of Santa Paula changed when my perspective changed.

In absolute reality, Santa Paula is too small and too big and just right, all of those things and none of those things, all at the same time. Santa Paula simply exists, it just is. Absolute reality is that place of unconditional "is-ness," a non-localized space that holds all realities—yet is independent of any one perception of reality.

Why is it important to understand the concept of absolute reality? Our understanding of the absolute helps us wonder about the proclamations we make. We can consider where we might treat our relative opinions like absolute truth. We can also ponder how our dogmatic clinging affects us. For most of us, our tenacious grasp of personal perspectives cuts us off from possibilities.

Everything in life is different than we think. We proclaim, "Santa Paula is too small," or "work is stressful," or "relationships are impossible," about external conditions. Or about ourselves, we say, "I am alone," "I am under-appreciated," or "I am fundamentally flawed." We say, "The world is falling apart," or "people are naturally selfish." But are these truths absolute? Do these truths require closer scrutiny? Perhaps our loaded, lauded perspectives about everything are only as solid as the size of Santa Paula.

The absolute stands in humble submission to our willingness to receive it through release of our relative truths. Our release may feel precarious at first, but ultimately, our willingness to let go and un-know allows us to be both empty and full at the same time. Letting go empties us of ego-imposed limitations as it fills us with endless possibilities.

And then there's Blondie. About 20 minutes into the goat hunt, I had an instinct to be still and know. I trusted nothing is ever lost in the infinite, for the infinite encompasses everything. I stood in the middle of the high school football field and prayed, "God, help me find Blondie."

I said "Amen," and two seconds later, my husband yelled, "Bon, I found her!" Blondie had convened an impromptu petting zoo in a neighbor's yard.

Our neighbors were delighted by the random goat visit. Blondie seemed proud of herself. She was the center of attention, there was a new lawn to conquer, and possibly a new case of explosive diarrhea to share. Hugh and I were relieved and happy to bring her home. The bonus for me was insight into the nature of reality. Blondie's escapade allowed me to explore a new awareness. For about 20 scary minutes, I fully inhabited the all-ness of being that reveals itself in missing goats, grass, explosive diarrhea, and small towns that suddenly turn big.

Later we moved Blondie to a farm in Ojai. There she played with other goats and undoubtedly charmed her new caretakers. I doubt she ever thought of herself as a great theologian. Yet, I will always treasure the excruciating moment when our holy goat led me to Rumi's field—a secret, sacred place where I devoured meaning beyond the relative; a place where I briefly grazed the hem of the garment of the unconditional absolute.

Reflections

Head: Where do you insist that your relative truths are the only truths?

Heart: Divine Love, release me from the limits of my opinions.

Hands: Abide in "Rumi's field." Notice where you argue for your opinion about yourself, others, and life. Let go just for a moment and stretch into another point of view. You don't have to live there—just try it on for size and see what happens.

Bonnie and Blondie The Holy Goat.

FREEING SENILE SACRED COWS

"When the Gods wish to punish us, they answer our prayers."

—Oscar Wilde

My experience with a holy goat inspired me to consider sacred cows. The phrase "sacred cow" is defined as a widely held idea or value that is incontrovertible. A sacred cow is steadfast and immune from questioning. All religions support a bonanza of sacred cows. Religions offer doctrines, dogmas, and practices some call absolute truth—even in my open-minded religion. Some of these sacred cows have gone senile. It's time to put them out to pasture and make room for deeper truths, longing to be known.

Shortly after we moved to Southern California, our cat Miranda (the understudy) discovered a long piece of plywood leaning up against our cinder block garden wall. Miranda used the board like a ramp to scale the wall and hide in our neighbor's yard. We were distraught when we realized she had escaped. We roamed the neighborhood and called her for hours, but she did not return. I stayed up all night worrying about her.

The next morning, the little hussy showed up at our front door and sashayed in to demand her breakfast. Hugh and I promptly eliminated her escape route. We moved the board away from the garden wall and propped it against a picnic table, so it led only to sky. When Miranda was ready to explore again, she returned to her board. The board was her sacred cow, her dogma, her path to freedom. But now, when she climbed it, she found it went nowhere. She glared at reality and meowed in righteous indignation because her cherished practice was no longer viable.

Many people start on a metaphysical path in search of freedom. We embark on an upward climb to liberate ourselves from perceived limitations, such as lack, poor health, or loneliness. I began my spiritual path when my acting teacher told me metaphysical principles would help me get performing jobs. I wanted to work in my chosen field. Performing was fun, plus I thought recognition as a singer/actor would fix me. Performing would free me from the bondage of perceived personal inadequacy. Getting cast in plays and operas would make me feel important, like one of the cool kids.

I read several "change your thinking, change your life" books. These books teach us how to create positive outcomes through the power of our thoughts. The books say the law of cause and effect and the Law of Attraction are always at work. Our minds initiate a process that transforms thoughts into things. If we become conscious about our thoughts, we can deliberately choose new ones, trusting better thoughts to create better outcomes. I learned everything I could on this topic. These spiritual laws became my sacred cows, and I herded them like I was one of the Cartwright boys. I clung to a belief that my use of an infallible spiritual law would fix my life. Through my ability to work the law, I would impress casting people, get hired, and be seen and accepted.

I put feet to my prayers and attended cattle-call auditions. I stood in endless lines of hundreds of other "female singers who move well." We waited in a rodeo chute, reluctant yet eager to be released into ubiquitous audition studios with beige walls and pale hardwood floors. Once there, we hoofed and mooed, that is we danced and sang for the casting people. Throughout the process, I flung positive intentions into the universe like lassos, hoping to hog-tie any job that would cure my insecurities. I was desperate to prove myself.

Sometimes my work with spiritual law was promising. After all, Miranda and I did cat affirmations for months and manifested the *Lettice and Lovage* tour. Other tools helped, too, and I was cast in some wonderful productions.

In general, understanding basic spiritual laws taught me to take responsibility for the contents of my mind. I learned my beliefs do have an impact on certain outcomes in life, and it felt good to have a sense of mastery over issues that once evoked feelings of hopelessness and helplessness.

However, sometimes my agenda went askew. My spiritual escape route from unwanted conditions felt like Miranda's board to nowhere. I failed to scale walls. I couldn't shake off the chains of personal inadequacy. I searched in vain for an inner *I Dream of Jeannie*, who could cross her arms and bob her ponytail to invoke the instant gratification of all my desires. But my efforts brought inconsistent results. Acting jobs refused to be hog-tied. Later I found myself running with scissors in a flailing church. Then I tried to pray away a tumor that stuck to my chest like a stubborn toad. My sacred cows were no longer mooing for me.

When the universe seems to deny our deepest desires, we often chastise ourselves for creating faulty outcomes. I wallowed in my inability to master the principles I was supposed to teach. I compared myself to others who "were doing it right." Like

Miranda, I meowed in a state of righteous indignation, railing against the universe's lack of cooperation with *my* needs.

When spiritual laws and sacred cows don't work, we may fret—or we can recognize the call of a deeper truth. We can trap ourselves in self-punishment—or we can enter into radiant curiosity. We can lament about our unfulfilled desires—or we can rest in the assurance of understanding a new heaven on earth.

Gradually I learned that failure to manifest has a purpose. It drives us from indignation to inspiration. For me, the road from indignation to inspiration was a path of exploration. I inspected my insides and saw my tendency to corral outdated, senile sacred cows—old truisms, spiritual laws I thought were supposed to work *my way* all the time. I realized I had a choice. I could choose to insist on my sacred cows and remain frustrated—or I could choose to be teachable. I chose teachable.

I asked questions such as, "Is it *always* appropriate to use spiritual law to *demand* material outcomes?" "Am I clinging to impermanent forms and results as sources of permanent well-being?" Or, "Will answered prayer according to *my* will offer me sustainable happiness? Could there be something better?" Through these questions, I discovered a new paradox: The spiritual laws I thought would bring me whatever I wanted in material results—sometimes worked best by not working.

I learned about the tendency to put the cart before the horse, or in my case, the cart before the senile sacred cow. That is, I looked at the tendency to reverse cause and effect. I was looking for jobs to fix my insecurities. I believed prestigious jobs would be the cause of my well-being. But soon I found performing jobs were like drugs. I'd get a job, a fix to make me feel good for a little while. Then the job would finish, the high would fade, and I'd be just as unsure and needful as I was when I started—perhaps even more so because now I had a reputation to uphold. The external world is effect. It is not cause. It will never "fix" us because we are not broken. Freedom happens when we release impermanent forms as the cause of our well-being. We become free as we rest in the true cause, that is, the heart of our true nature.

Our inner divine nature is cause. It has been with us always. Our divine nature gives us everything. It alone has the capacity to witness and befriend the ego. Its benevolence transforms ranting insecurities into sacred security. It abides in faith and urges us to discover how skillfully managed manifestation-fails bring us what we *really* want. For behind all longing for material forms is a longing for God—the innermost, highest God that is pure loving awareness.

Once we become secure in our true divine identity, we may or may not experience results in the world of form. But as soon as we immerse ourselves in truth, external proof of our worthiness no longer matters. The causal power we once gave to external conditions falls away.

Alignment with pure awareness is enough. Self-acceptance and well-being flourish in all circumstances. We fall in love with everything as everything seemingly falls in love with us. A dynamic mystery overtakes us, and we thrive in unconditional freedom.

This is the deeper meaning of "change your thinking, change your life." Become unconditional. See the false self as a necessary, mischievous, yet well-meaning illusion—an illusion that gives us something to do, that keeps us interested and alert. But refrain from over-identifying with the illusion. Detach from dependency on outcomes. Align with the divine and allow her to become your mentor. Divine Love will provide you with unconditional joy in all conditions.

We do not have to wait to be free. We do not need material results to bring us happiness. Our true nature is free and happy now because it sees beyond the chain-linked beliefs of the ego. The happiness and freedom we seek has already sought and found us. When we bind ourselves to this boundless truth—paradoxically, this binding sets us free.

Bonnie backstage at the opera, circa 1995.

Reflections

Head: Have you ever received blessings through unanswered prayers?

Heart: Divine Love, bind me to boundless truth. Set me free.

Hands: Notice how you make outer conditions responsible for inner well-being. Look for the spiritual value behind the desired conditions – love, joy, peace, or other. Then receive that value by offering it to another being.

THE EXULTATION OF THE UNCONDITIONAL

"Between stimulus and response there is a space. In that space is our power to choose our response. In our response lies our growth and our freedom."
—Viktor E. Frankl

How does unconditional being help us navigate life? Many years ago when I worked as a psychiatric nurse, I had a girl fight with one of the therapists. We didn't physically hurt each other, but we hurled many snark-infested missiles back and forth. After 20 minutes of verbal wrestling, we couldn't resolve our differences. Both of us left the exchange feeling hurt and angry.

My husband came home to find me crying on our living room couch. I told him the story of the girl fight. I'm sure I emphasized my friend's role in creating the unpleasant exchange, while downplaying my responsibility. He listened for a while and then he said, "You know, you don't have to be at the effect of her cause."

I looked at him like he was speaking in tongues. I had never heard of such a thing.

"Huh?" I said.

"You don't have to be at the effect of her cause."

"What in the name of sweet holy Jesus does that even mean?" I asked.

"Her hurtful words don't have to hurt you," he replied.

"Oh."

I had always believed if someone was mean to me, my hurt, disappointment, fear, and anger was mandatory—just a fact of life.

I woke my husband up several times in the middle of the night to say, "Hey, Hugh, what was that thing you said about cause and effect?" He patiently repeated, "You don't have to be at the effect of her cause."

It took a while, but gradually I started to understand I could step back from arguments and other challenges; overcome my knee jerk reactions; and choose better ways of responding to whatever was happening. I didn't have to take anything personally, or "be at the effect of someone else's cause." I could cause—that is, take responsibility for—my own reactions.

This practice made me less susceptible to the manipulations of those who wanted to dictate what I should feel. Sometimes people want you to feel badly because they feel badly. They may gnaw at you until you get as hurt or angry as they are. They may accuse you of being careless or insensitive if you react calmly. They may bully you with anger or guilt.

I got bullied big time at the start of COVID. Just as the mask mandates were coming into being, I went to Starbucks. I wore a mask and stood six feet away from the person who was at the cash register placing his order. He was not wearing a mask, his body language was chaotic, and I could tell he struggled with boundaries. He swaggered against the counter and bellowed a long dissertation to the barista on the tragic chemicals embedded in the sweeteners Starbucks offered. I could tell that the polite barista was eager for him to leave; plus, I was impatient for my caffeine fix. So I attempted a tactful fake cough. The unmasked man turned around and started coughing *on me*. Then he began yelling.

"Don't you fake-cough on me, you stupid bitch."

I raised my eyebrows and half-smiled, so he continued.

"I'm gonna find out where your mother lives and kill her."

"My mother's already dead," I said.

"Then I'll kill your daughter," he bellowed.

"But I don't have any children," I replied.

He yelled a few more outlandish threats at me. My only response was a gentle comment: "Your name is Grumpy McGrumperson today." That made him even madder. But when my outrage didn't rise to the level he required, he left me alone.

I got to the counter and told the barista, "I guess I need to work on my fake cough."

This guy's behavior was puzzling instead of painful, so it was easy to practice non-attachment. It's often more challenging to keep sane and well-bounded in subtler exchanges, but I do think of this man often. He taught me about the power of staying unconditionally aligned with who I want to be in the face of comments designed to derail me.

Our kind, ethical treatment of living beings is important, but ultimately we are not responsible for others' feelings or reactions. When our boundaries and perceptions of personal responsibility become clearer, our relationships get better. It helps to remember we all contain an impenetrable inner place. When we connect to this place, we can respond to others with poise and compassion.

As we become less available to the manipulation of others, we become less likely to manipulate. We allow people to be who they are without imposing our personal needs or agendas on them. Our willingness to refrain from manipulating others impacts others' ability to manipulate us, and vice versa. We become free as we set others free. Then we all enjoy greater response-ability with less reactivity.

As for my girl fight with the therapist, within days we apologized, forgave, and became friends again. I know our forgiveness was complete, because I was grateful for our hostile exchange—grateful to learn about reactivity and response-ability. Grateful to learn I didn't have to be at the effect of anyone's cause. And grateful to learn no one needs to be at the effect of *my* cause. I could be unconditional and offer others that same grace.

Deeper gratitude emerged when I learned this teaching about cause, effect, and unconditional living applies to our relationship with life. We do not need to be at the effect of *life's* cause. We can remain unconditional. Our happiness, freedom, peace, and joy are never tarnished or bound by conditions.

Gandhi's wife, Kasturba, was imprisoned many times for her participation in non-violent protests. When a journalist asked her, "How do you feel about going to prison?" Kasturba replied, "There is no prison." Prison could not affect Kasturba's freedom. She was not at the effect of her jailer's cause. She was not a victim of circumstance, so her inner freedom remained intact even when she was locked in a cell with iron bars.

Viktor Frankl was confined to a German concentration camp where the Nazi soldiers sought to break his body and spirit. Frankl learned to transcend suffering though finding meaning in his life circumstances. He developed a philosophy that taught others to live in deeper meaning. He taught us about the space between stimulus and response; and how that sacred space allows us to *choose* a response that leads to growth and freedom. Frankl transcended the Nazi's cause and proved that conditions cannot kill consciousness.

My early challenges in the church couldn't diminish me. My touch of cancer could not sabotage my joy. I didn't always know this *during* the challenges, but now, with the gift of hindsight, I try and remember everything happens to support our growth in love. We don't have to let circumstances define us. Instead, we can define circumstances.

The way to define circumstances is to cultivate the willingness to be with things as they are. This is not resignation. It is non-resistance, creative empowerment that easily becomes resiliency. We notice what is happening. We welcome it. We say, "My true unassailable self is greater than this condition." We see all conditions as teachers, as opportunities to choose anew. This moves us into the *exultation* of the unconditional. And strangely—or not—when we become joyfully unconditional, we make better choices. Then conditions improve. Another paradox.

We thrive and life becomes gratitude. We say: "Thank you, Divine Love. Thank you for inviting the infinite expand-ability of consciousness through me. Thank you for everything that provides an on-ramp to a plane of jubilant growth. Thank you for illuminating the freedom to celebrate whatever life offers. Thank you for expansive grace. And thank you for an amazing life, even when it isn't, all the time."

Reflections

Head: Where are you at the effect of cause? What situations upset you? Is your response mandatory?

Heart: Divine Love, inspire me to live unconditionally in the spaciousness where miracles abound.

Hands: Practice non-resistance. Monitor your reactivity versus your response-ability today with people and circumstances. Find the inner equanimity that is greater than unwanted conditions. You don't have to put up with what is unwanted—but you can back away or set loving boundaries with a sense of poised, creative empowerment.

WHO LICKED THE VET?

"Look at God looking at you...and smiling."
—Anthony De Mello

Back to the vet encounter. As you may recall, I was obsessed with licking the vet. In the midst of a boil lancing procedure, with two dogs, the vet, and me, the good doctor stopped abruptly and complained about "too many tongues in the room." I panicked and prayed I was not the perpetrator.

After his comment about "too many tongues," the vet said, "Let's bring Bartie to the back to get his nails clipped." Bartie went for his pedicure. The vet sucked the pus out of Stella's boil. There was no more unsolicited licking, yet my tongue still went home with its tail between its legs.

That was the last time I thought about licking the actual vet. The urge shifted to one of his female technicians while taking Stella's temperature. "Do clients ever lick you and blame their animal?" I asked. The vet tech backed away slowly and we never spoke of it again. Until now.

The moral of this story is my pervasive thoughts did not create a particular physical outcome at the vet's office. My thoughts created a shift in *my* consciousness, an inner climate of anxiety plus comedy. But I wasn't the one who got sent to the back office for a pedicure. In terms of the *physical* manifestation of the vet-tonguing, I'm pretty sure Bartie was the licker.

This scenario added to my ponderings about manifestation and "creating our own reality through the power of our thoughts." The idea of creating reality is probably true in part. We certainly create our perception of reality through the content of our beliefs. But now I wonder: *Who is the "I" that creates? Is it my ego? Or does this separate self, this illusion, work in concert with something greater—something that embraces yet transcends the ego? Is all deliberate creation an opportunity to awaken to the consciousness of the great one, the I Am presence that creates on behalf of all beings, through each of us?*

After years of spiritual study and experience, I now trust the Law of Attraction is also a law of awakening. It is joyful to "attract" things or "manifest" changed conditions. It's part of what we're here to experience. However, we don't need to cling to the manifestation of matter as the source of our well-being. There is no need to boost our control, security, or approval ratings with props and accolades. Our lives become great when we awaken to the inner kingdom of heaven embedded in the here and now. When we awaken to the essence of the unconditional absolute that dwells in everything, we are invincible. The illusions of fear and separation fall away and life is an exquisite blessing.

As we practice the Law of Attraction, which is a law of awakening, we also practice a law of alignment. We align with our true nature. When we align, we embody the qualities of the divine, such as love, peace, happiness, and harmony. This shift in embodied alignment is the answer to all prayers.

I don't claim to have the skills to describe the state of embodied alignment in the unconditional absolute. I'm no holy goat. But I do know we each have our personal mode of knowing when we are aligned. For me, the greatest barometer of alignment is joy. When I am joyful, I feel the presence of God.

That's what happened at the vet's office on that fateful day. The one consciousness needed a laugh. I'm willing to bet that like me, God is always ready for a good time. So the divine sought a willing participant to help her have fun. She found me and planted an unorthodox vet-licking mantra in my head.

Then she lined up the actors. She assembled a neck boil, two frisky dogs, and a kind veterinarian. She shoved us into an unruly wrestling match on a cold linoleum floor. She laughed out loud when I panicked over the potential lick. She gazed adoringly at a timeless metaphor for life—the endless collision of humanity with divinity in an infinite intimate space. As always, she reveled in the comedy of human-divine existence.

That's my story and I'm sticking to it. I thrive in the kingdom of unconditional joy. When this reality tempts me, I will not hold my tongue.

Reflections

Head: Does your God have a sense of humor? What are some examples of God's funny bone?

Heart: Divine Love, help me find comedy in being human.

Hands: Look for the comedy of the universe wherever you go. Allow God to have a good time through you. See if you can help someone smile today.

PART SIX:

DANCING IN SUFFERING AND JOY

KNOW NOTHING, TRUST EVERYTHING

"Faith is taking the first step even when you don't see the whole staircase."
—Martin Luther King Jr.

Our dog, Stella, sat hunched on the worn green and white armchair in my home office. The chair cradled her as she tracked me with perplexed eyes. I packed for a two-week spiritual pilgrimage to Chennai, India. She didn't like it. I didn't like it either. Because something had gone wrong during the night.

Hugh was out of town. I went to bed early to get a good sleep before my 30-hour trip to the other side of the world. In the middle of the night, I heard a rasping sound and felt the bed shake. I looked to my left and saw Stella on the bed beside me poised like a Sphinx, breathing loud and fast.

It's anxiety, I thought. *She probably knows I'm leaving tomorrow.*

The next day at 6 a.m. her breathing was still wrong. This wasn't anxiety. This was bad. Even her Vizsla-brother, Bartie, knew as he whimpered and leaned on my leg.

My open suitcase on the blue rug was an abyss in front of

Stella's chair. Should I fill it? No, first I had to count dog respirations. Still too fast. *Maybe give her a little space,* I thought. So I staggered barefoot on the hardwood floor to the bedroom. I jerked white clothes for the ashram out of my closet and attempted a casual stroll back down the hall. I shoved the clothes into my suitcase, then checked Stella's breathing again. No change.

It was too early to call the vet. *Check the internet,* I thought, *maybe Google will offer hope.* There was good news—it could be a lung infection—and with antibiotics, she's better. But there was bad news, too—possible lung cancer and other horrifying dog diseases.

I sat at my computer with my head in my hands. *This can't be happening,* I thought. *What should I do? Could I get on a plane and leave my best friend? The trip is paid for, a gift from my church. I can't disappoint them.*

Then I thought, *This could be nothing. I'm paranoid about the dogs. What if I stay home and she's fine? Google said she might be okay.* Then I flip-flopped back to, *What if she's not okay? What if she dies? What kind of a greedy, people-pleasing, dog-abandoning wretch am I?*

I paced, stared at Stella, and continued to pack. As I did, I remembered I didn't even want to go to India. I remembered the conversation I had with Hugh two months ago, the day I made this unholy decision.

That morning, I came into our bedroom and saw Hugh asleep on our king-sized bed, tangled in an antique ivory quilt. Stella and Bartie shared the bed with him. Stella curled beside him like a red cinnamon bun. Bartie stretched out his stiff arms and legs in what we call the piano bench position.

"Hey. Hugh," I whispered loudly.

I pulled the shade and the morning light streamed into the bedroom. I sat beside him and gently shook his shoulder.

He opened one sleep-encrusted eye and asked, "What?"

"I think I'm going to India."

That got his attention.

"Seriously?" he replied, turning over to face me.

"I got this email," I said. "There's a seminar with a bunch of spiritual leaders. It's about awakening to love. I ignored it three times, but I think I'm supposed to go."

"You won't like India."

He had a point. Hugh lived in India in the 1970s near Sri Aurobindo's ashram. He knew I didn't like to travel, and that India might not appeal to my suburban sensibilities.

"I have 10 reasons why I shouldn't go," I said.

"Such as?"

"Thirty hours on a plane. Poverty. I don't know if I can take it."

"My mother cried for days when she visited," he said.

"And I drink a ton of water."

"You can't," he replied.

"I know," I said, imagining amoebic dysentery and adult diapers.

"So why?" he asked.

"I don't know…maybe a new perspective? Maybe to get a better understanding of God…or to help me be a better minister somehow? That's what logic says, but it's more. There's something I can't name. My brain says, 'stay at home,' but my body feels pulled—every cell dragging me into the unknown. Is it grandiose to say it feels like God's calling me? That I've been summoned by the Holy Spirit without knowing why? I don't like it. I really don't like it. But this feels real."

He nodded. We've both learned to recognize the divine voice

that challenges us to grow. In that moment, I made the decision to go, based on trust.

Now it felt like God was screwing with me. Again. Okay, I was called to India. Maybe. There was no skywriting that said, "Go to India, you complacent twit." Okay, I was supposed to trust. Maybe. But going to India for personal growth and inspiration was one thing. Going when my dog might be dying was insulting. It was a horror story with no happy ending in sight. I had to choose. I could choose God's sketchy agenda or loyalty to my dog—my dog who offered me tangible evidence of unconditional love every day for 11 years. Would I choose God or choose Stella?

I didn't know what to do. So I kept moving. I finished packing. Bug-spray, flip-flops, anti-poop medicine in the suitcase. I forced myself into the shower where I sobbed, wrenching body spasms shearing my courage.

Why did she have to get sick now? What if she dies? God, what should I do? I'll do whatever you want, just tell me.

An inner voice nudged, "*Ask for help.*"

Ask who? I wondered.

I got out of the shower, got dressed, and checked Stella. No change.

Grant, our teenage pet sitter, arrived. I told him about Stella's condition and together we asked for help. We contacted our friend, Becky, who promised she would take Stella to the vet as soon as the clinic opened.

I made the decision to go, maybe not to India, but at least to the airport. Then I said good-bye—good-bye for now, or good-bye forever.

I cradled Stella's butterscotch face in my hands. She leaned in as I lingered and smelled her earthy coat. I kissed the top of her bony head and whispered, "Will I ever see you again?" Then I pried my hands away and put my sunglasses on so Grant wouldn't see me cry. I backed out the door and stumbled to my car to drive five miles to the airport shuttle where I would meet my travel companions, Marc, Greg, Lida, and Carol. I abandoned Stella for India.

Reflections

Head: What impossible decisions have you faced? How do you discern what to do in the face of deep uncertainty?

Heart: Divine Love, please help me receive your guidance in all things.

Hands: Amplify your capacity to trust life. Notice how many acts of trust you participate in every day—driving on the freeway, trusting your body's ability to digest food, trusting the skill and kindness of others, and more.

32

PRAYERS ON A PLANE

"Prayer does not change God, but it changes the one who prays."

—Søren Kierkegaard

It's a two-hour drive from Ventura County to Los Angeles International Airport. While I was in the shuttle, Becky took Stella to the vet. She called as I arrived at LAX and said, "The vet isn't sure what's going on with Stella. He thinks it may be lung metastasis from a hidden tumor. He'll X-ray her lungs again in two weeks when you get back."

Two weeks: magic words. The vet thought Stella would survive two weeks; he thought I should get on the plane.

I paused at the threshold. Inside the plane, a flight attendant wearing a teal dress and perky hat chirped "good morning." Behind me, a pierced Asian teenager in baggy black clothes plopped down his over-stuffed backpack as I hesitated. I took one step back and bumped into him. He scowled at me, and I apologized.

A teenager's impatience and a little shove from my friend, Marc, propelled me on board. The line of passengers closed in behind me and it was done. There was no turning back unless I wanted to swim upstream in the aisle. I was trapped until our first stop in Hong Kong where I could call home again.

Make the best of it, I said. *Be strong. Do what's expected.*

I found my seat, a grey polyester prison for the next 15 hours. I climbed to my place by the window and shoved my laptop under the seat in front of me. Marc took the middle seat beside me. I took off my hiking shoes and fastened my seat belt. The other passengers drifted to their seats and the door of the plane snapped shut like the lid of a coffin. Nothing to do but wait and hate myself for leaving.

I leaned my forehead against the cool glass of the window. *Try not to think about Stella,* I thought. *Distract yourself with in-flight movies. This one with Bruce Willis and lots of explosions looks good.*

I watched the Bruce Willis movie. I paused every half hour or so to scrutinize our trek across the Pacific on the seat back monitor in front of me. The monitor showed a primitive gold image of a plane that crept across a black screen like an injured turtle. I willed it to move faster, but it didn't cooperate. I watched another movie, a comedy. The flight attendant brought vegetarian gruel and basmati rice. I tried to eat, but couldn't. I checked the turtle on the monitor again. Half an inch. I watched a third movie as I inhaled the smell of curry and sweaty feet. Enough. I tried to sleep.

When I didn't sleep, I raised the window shade and stared into blackness. I couldn't watch another movie. I couldn't get away from myself. I lost my resolve and collapsed into longing for Stella with a dog-sized hole in my heart.

I began to cry. I was quiet, wiping my eyes and nose on the sleeve of my turquoise hoodie. I felt Marc stir beside me.

Marc blinked his eyes open.

"Oh honey," he said.

"No seriously, I'm terrific," I sniffled as I rolled my eyes.

"I know." Marc said. "But tell me."

"This sucks. It just sucks." I stamped my foot as best I could with limited legroom.

"It does suck." Marc said. "I know how much you love her. It was probably love at first sight, right?"

I told Marc my Stella stories—how we got her, the items she chewed as a puppy, the tampon jubilee. I spoke about her training—show, agility, and obedience, all brightened by her skill and stubbornness. I told him of hand-made dog costumes, first a hot pink poodle skirt, then the Native American couture.

I told how I stood in the dairy aisle at Vons, memorizing the attire of the now politically incorrect Land-O-Lakes Butter woman so I could recreate the look and impose it on Stella. That day, there were many serious grown-up things to do. Instead, I sewed faux-indigenous fringe on Naugahyde and braided a black yarn wig that she would shred in 45 seconds.

I reminded him I quit a lucrative corporate job to work in a church full-time.

"I did it to devote more time to Stella," I said. "Was that stupid?"

Marc reminded me about how we talked when I decided to serve at a church because it would make my dog happy.

"You remember what I told you at the time?" he asked.

"Yeah, you said God uses ridiculous bait to get us to go where we're needed. I took a risk because of Stella. And when it was so hard at the beginning, I stayed because of her. And now the church is beautiful. People's lives change. So much good has happened in that crazy church because my dog forced me to stay."

"An amazing girl," Marc said, referring to Stella.

"I know," I sobbed.

"We love each other," I continued. "She follows me everywhere. She sits beside me and puts her head on my shoulder when we're in the car. She sleeps under the covers, curled up against me like one of those Russian nesting dolls."

I got louder, crying more.

"And we're not only nested physically," I said. "We're nested emotionally. My heart wraps around her heart. I'm here to protect her. But today I'm on a plane to freaking India when she needs me most. And I promised her, Marc. I promised! I promised I'd be with her at the end!"

Full-blown crying now, tears streaming down my face, not even bothering to wipe my nose, I covered my eyes with my hands and allowed the grief to consume me.

According to the monitor, we were over the Pacific Ocean, about halfway to Hong Kong. We could have been on Pluto. There was nothing resembling life, no twinkling lights below, no stars, no warmth, no comfort—just infinite darkness. Just me and my cramped grief wrapped in an airline-quality blanket. There was no place to go, nothing to be done, no solution in sight. I couldn't take it anymore. I had to get away from the pain. I didn't know what to do but I had to do something.

I told Marc to go back to sleep. And I prayed.

I prayed silently, begging God, *Please God, please, please keep Stella safe until I get back. Don't let her die alone. I'll do whatever you want. I'll stop swearing, I'll be nicer to telemarketers, I'll stop with the vet licking business, I'll be a better person. Just let her live.*

I watched myself forage through my character flaws, like a bargain bin in a flea market. I was willing to renounce anything for answered prayer. My halo tarnished and crumbled as I heard echoes of what I tell my congregation. Things like, "Don't bargain with God…Become unconditional…Prayer isn't about changing God's mind. We pray to change *our* hearts," or "The best prayer is '*Thy will be done*'."

I had been a platitude-spewing fraud. A hypocrite. I didn't

give a flying flea-market about God's will. Because this was different. This was about *my* pain. I demanded an instant cure, and a sign Stella would be safe.

I prayed harder but didn't feel any better. My shoulders crept up to my earlobes. My hands twisted in my lap. My head hurt. I wanted to pound my fists on the seatback of the sleeping passenger in front of me.

Eventually, either exhaustion or grace overtook me—because just for an instant, I stopped trying to bend God's will. I breathed deeply three or four times. My shoulders relaxed and I prayed again: *Okay God, I give up. Thy will be done. Change my heart. Please.*

I waited. At first only silence. Then a small, new thought grew within me.

What if it's selfish to cling to Stella? What if she's suffering? What if she's on her own path, separate from my need? What if real love is letting go?

I didn't like it. I didn't want to believe I *could* let go. But I was willing to consider what was best for Stella.

Something deeper unraveled. My heart expanded like a dove stretching her wings. I remembered telling Marc how Stella and I were like Russian nesting dolls—how I wrapped around her warm body when she slept beside me in bed; how my heart wrapped around her heart; how my care enfolded her well-being, always.

Suddenly, I gasped and sat up straight and thought, *Wait, I take care of Stella, right? What if all this time, Stella has been taking care of me?*

Tears of recognition leapt into my eyes.

It's true, I thought. *Stella is my hero, my protector—making me laugh when it's impossible to laugh, bringing me to my amazing church, comforting me, walking beside me, and loving me in all my flawed wonder. She is my guardian, my angel, my stand in for God's love. And this love has taken care of me always.*

Even now, an inner voice whispered.

Even now? I thought. *Even in the desperate timing of Stella's illness colliding with an essential trip to India—this is love, too?*

Yes.

I began to cry again, but this time for the holiness of what was happening.

The plane that had once seemed like a coffin was now a cloister. I felt something new, something sacred. I couldn't define it, couldn't understand it yet. But I was willing to learn, willing to allow God to change my heart.

I thought back to the conversation I had with my husband months ago, when he asked, "Why do you want to go to India?"

I didn't know the answer when he asked, but I did now. It was for this. It was to cry and remember. It was to hold a vigil of unknowing. It was to pray in the darkness to fly into absolute light. It was to know that here, in this hallowed plane, I could know nothing and trust everything.

Reflections

Head: Where have you faced uncertainty and acted on faith? What helps you know what to do?

Heart: Divine Love, help me accept your highest will in all things.

Hands: Notice where you bargain with God. Then ask God to change your heart. If you're able, back up your changed heart with an action.

33
HOLDING ON AND LETTING GO

"Some people believe holding on and hanging in there are signs of great strength. However, there are times when it takes much more strength to know when to let go and then do it."

—Ann Landers

The trip to India was a pilgrimage.

I kept my watch set on California time, 12-and-a-half hours behind India. For the entire journey, I mentally straddled darkness and light. India was amazing and Stella inhabited every moment. Joy and sorrow mingled like paints on a palate to create something different, a color unknown to me until then. Despite my dying dog, or *because* of my dying dog, a new grace awakened within me. The more I surrendered, the more I fell in love; the more I fell in love, the more I surrendered. I was a willing captive in God's mystery.

After two weeks of travel and limited phone and internet connection, I returned home. I wondered what I would find. Would Stella be alive? When I arrived, Hugh flung open the front door of our house. "Mommy's home," he said.

Two dogs, Bartie and Stella, bounded to my side.

Stella bounded slowly. She was still sick and clearly dying. Her breathing was still too fast, and she needed help to jump up on the bed. The next day, we went back to our vet and then a specialist. No one could figure out what was wrong with her. The doctors offered to do more medical tests. When I learned whatever she had was probably cancer in her lungs and liver, I said, "Enough." All she ever wanted was to be near me. I couldn't hospitalize her for more tests that would cause physical pain plus the pain of separation.

Hugh suggested I take her to the beach one last time.

It was a grey morning at low tide. There were a few Asian fishermen on the beach and a flock of sandpipers. We walked by a jetty and sat on the cool sand. Then we cascaded into the canine version of *Our Town*, where Emily says good-bye to her life on earth.

Stella and I said good-bye to 11 years of beach runs. Good-bye to late afternoons, pink sunsets, low tides, and polished English toffee-colored sand. Good-bye to pointing at "birdies" and bouncing neon tennis balls; good-bye to our proud muscular dog leaping high to catch them. Good-bye to demented rolling in rotting seals, red legs flailing upward in stinking joy. Good-bye to Stella sticking her head in a picnicker's Dorito's bag and scarfing a fisherman's hamburger before I could stop her.

I whispered to her, to prepare her for her next adventure. I kissed her rusty cheek and said, "Maybe when you're gone, you won't really be gone, you'll just be invisible. Maybe when you're invisible, you'll get to go more places with me—like Macy's, or the DMV." I didn't know if it was true, but I said it anyway.

Behind the soothing words, despite my change of heart on the plane to India, I couldn't believe this was happening. It was too soon. I wanted three more years. I backslid into my own agenda. I momentarily let go of the "thy will be done" business, and proclaimed, "It is done unto you as you believe. You can fix this, Bonnie." I prayed for a cure and clutched at Jesus, Buddha, Krishna—anyone who could help. Soon I was begging for this undiagnosable illness to back off.

Then I shook my head as I thought of the many times I've comforted people facing death and other humiliations. I considered the prayers and platitudes I've offered, and I sighed into the futility of what we do in our never-ending fight with impermanence. I sat broken-hearted, immersed in the insistent stampede of mortality.

It may be wrong to compare me and my dying dog to the Pietà, that beautiful image of Mother Mary holding Jesus, her broken, beloved son after the crucifixion. But that's who I was on the barren beach that day. I was Stella's mother. Stella was my savior, my child, my North Star, my love. Because of that love, I saw again, I had to give up the illusion of control and let her go.

And because I could only let go, I held her as tightly as I could, and then we went home.

Reflections

Head: When have you been reluctant to let go and let God?

Heart: Divine Love, teach me when to let go and when to hold on.

Hands: Take a few moments to imagine it is your last day. What precious good-byes would you say? Can you express the love today, that abides in these eventual good-byes?

VULNERABILITY—BLESSING OR CURSE?

"The truth will set you free, but first it will make you miserable."
—James A. Garfield

Once I got home, I immediately picked up *my* will again and started rummaging for signs Stella would live. Every morning I asked her, "Can you walk, sweetheart?" If she walked from the bedroom to the kitchen, that would mean a cure was possible.

Stella didn't want to move. I grabbed a piece of hamburger, held it under her nose, and lured her off the bed. She wobbled down the hall to the kitchen where I encouraged her to eat the white rice and ground beef I cooked for her. She sniffed, ate a few bites, then stared at the kitchen door contemplating the effort required to go outside and pee.

We walked to the back yard and Stella faltered. Again I asked, loudly and sweetly, "Can you walk?"

I didn't care who heard me: Hugh, through the open windows of his office, staring at his computer and concerned about both of us; the neighbors next door who once yelled at Stella for barking. They would know she was weak, and I was no longer the feisty smart-ass who yelled back at them. I didn't care. I was willing to expose my heartache and speak the foreign language of vulnerability.

In my family of origin, vulnerability was rare. It was okay to cry during sentimental movies and great music. Happy tears at weddings were okay, sad tears at funerals, not so much. We were strong, descendants of stoic German immigrants. Our German ancestors left a legacy that taught us to be unflappable, capable, and positive—no matter what. Vulnerability looked like weakness to us and that was unacceptable.

My mother was diagnosed with cancer when I was 13. She became ill quickly, and although there were good times during my teen years, she was often in the hospital, undergoing chemotherapy, surgery, or radiation. Near the end, she was in a bed in our living room, wearing a wig and getting morphine injections.

My older sisters went to college or started careers. I was left behind to finish high school sandwiched between my parents and a deep sense of foreboding. We never had an open conversation about my mother's illness. She was everything to our family, and a talk about losing her would be too real. It would undo us.

When I was small, every year at the end of summer vacation we visited Playland, an amusement park in Rye, New York. Amusement parks weren't common back then, so this was special. My sisters and I looked forward to our trip all summer long. One year when I was about five, I told one of my stuffed animals—a small, brown, threadbare dog named Snappy—he could come with us.

My father worked long hours in Manhattan, so my mother was responsible for the family outing. She packed her four daughters into our blue 1960's station wagon, and set off for

Playland, about 45 minutes away. We were almost there when I realized I was missing someone.

"Mommy!" I wailed, "I forgot Snappy."

I held in my tears because I didn't want my big sisters to think I was a baby. Everyone in the car felt my distress and my sisters were fit to be tied. Their attitude was something like, "Suck it up, kid, we're not turning around."

My mother got off the freeway and took us back home to get my stuffed animal. When my wicked sisters (whom I love dearly) objected, my mother said, "She's been promising him all week." End of story. We got Snappy, drove back to Playland, and had a great time.

My sisters don't remember that incident. They don't remember their frigid response to my pain. These days, I enjoy teasing them about it and they respond with equanimity—and with reverence for our mother, the warm-hearted, *undoubtedly* fatigued woman who turned the car around. The one who faced the disdain of the big girls, because her littlest girl made a promise to a toy. A love like that is precious and hard to find. A love like that is even harder to lose.

The thought of losing my mother terrified me, so I became quiet when she got sick. I wouldn't consider a life without her, so I didn't ask questions like, "Can you walk, sweetheart?" as I did with Stella. I wanted to ask my mother, "Are you going to die?" But I didn't because I secretly knew the answer, and the answer would change everything.

Her cancer grew worse during my senior year of high school. Then shortly before my 18th birthday, it seemed death was close. Not that we talked about it. We never mentioned how the cancer was devouring her bones and internal organs, how it was planning to steal my favorite person. We didn't talk about the undoing of my mother's dreams, how she would never see her four girls grow into gracious women.

I didn't talk about my fear of loss—what her death would take from me. I refused to consider coming home from college without her eager face waiting for me at the kitchen window. Or how she wouldn't be there to cherish every detail of my new life and confirm the best of my being.

On my mother's last day, I was alone with her in our living room. She couldn't speak coherently, yet she wanted to tell me something. Maybe she wanted to remedy the years of suppressed communication, or to warn me of impending death, or maybe she wanted my help. At that moment I desperately *wanted* to talk, to know the truth, because I wanted to save her. *I'm only 17*, I thought. *What should I do? I need to fix this.*

In the absence of any remedy, I sat beside her and held her hand. My tears flowed as I waited, bewildered in the face of an unthinkable ending. Then perhaps in one last act of selflessness, my mother suddenly became alert. She looked at me and said, "Thank you." Those were the last words she ever said to me.

She died 12 hours later. The undertakers came and took her body away in a black bag. Again, I didn't know what to do. *How can I learn to talk about her in the past tense?* I wondered. *How can I live without the person who loves me most; the person who turned the car around on the way to Playland, the one who sacrificed approval and convenience for extravagant love?*

I had all these thoughts—yet held them close. I didn't want anyone to see my pain. I thought people would pity me. They would worry and then I would become a burden.

So I pretended I was fine. I proceeded with my college plans, cleaned the house for my father, and refused to grieve. I went out with my friends at night and drank too much with my fake ID. I plowed through to-do lists and social engagements wearing the armor of self-protection. I didn't know where this path of rigidity would lead, but I was unwilling to change my direction.

Unlike my mother, I couldn't take a risk. I couldn't turn the car around for love.

Reflections

Head: How vulnerable are you willing to be?

Heart: Divine Love, please help me know that what I once called weakness is really strength.

Hands: Try vulnerability. Ask a hard question of yourself and listen to the answer with compassion.

35

SUFFERING IS THE NEW JOY

"Why love, if losing hurts so much? I have no answers anymore: only the life I have lived. Twice in that life I've been given the choice: as a boy and as a man. The boy chose safety, the man chooses suffering. The pain now is part of the happiness then. That's the deal."

—C.S. Lewis

It was 37 years after my mother died. Stella approached death, and I wondered if I could be fully present with my grief. Had I learned anything through the years of nursing, operas, living, dying, and ministry? Was there a place where I could feel pain, yet love completely? Could I metaphorically turn the car around and stray from the path of unflinching stoicism? Could I ask hard questions—like "Can you walk?"—and love the answers no matter what? Could I learn to suffer?

My first cautious steps toward suffering happened in New York in the 1990s. I was an understudy in the Broadway production of *Shadowlands*. The play is about C.S. Lewis's transition from intellect to experience. When Lewis was a child, his mother died. He never cried, never allowed himself to feel the loss. Like me, he probably didn't ask the hard questions. Then late in life, when Lewis was a sedate bachelor professor, he met his true love, Joy Gresham. Shortly after they married, Joy got cancer and died. When his wife died, Lewis allowed grief to overtake him.

In the play, Lewis said, "*The boy chose safety, the man chooses suffering.*" Eight shows a week, sitting backstage listening to the monitors, I heard those words: *The boy chose safety, the man chooses suffering.*

In my remaining days with Stella, I chose suffering. It was an impeccable choice.

Suffering can be a hard sell. In the early days of my metaphysical training, I learned we should strive to create a life without suffering. "You can learn all of your life lessons in joyful, gentle ways," my teachers told me.

I encounter people who say, "Pain is inevitable, suffering is optional." The folks who offer this wisdom often imply if your pain causes suffering, you're doing something wrong. They say, "Suffering is pain plus resistance." Then there are certain non-dual teachers who tell us suffering indicates subjection to the ego, the separate self. As I went deeper into mysticism, I accepted a new view of suffering.

Shadowlands planted a seed. Later I encountered authors such as Father Richard Rohr, who wrote of an alternative orthodoxy where "The path of descent is the path of transformation. Darkness, failure, relapse, death, and woundedness are our primary teachers, rather than ideas or doctrines." Fr. Rohr says the two most important portals for growth are great love and great suffering.

Then to the non-dual teachers who say suffering is evidence of the separate self, I learned to say, "Yes, and…" Ralph Waldo Emerson wrote, "Only the finite has wrought and suffered. The infinite lies stretched in smiling repose." Some offer this as evidence that suffering equals duality, immersion in the finite self; but I believe this statement has layers.

All beings are both finite and infinite. Non-duality has no opposite. Non-duality *includes* the *perception* of duality. The illusion of a separate self is an integral part of the human-divine experience—and sometimes the illusion *seems* to writhe and suffer.

Emily Hess, September 17, 1925 - July 8, 1976.

But through process, paradox, and the appearance of suffering, the illusory finite self extends a portal to the possibility of infinite gifts—gifts beyond logical comprehension and gifts too beautiful to behold. Suffering means allowing—staying present with what is. In this place of presence, we do not heap the shame of "doing something wrong" on top of suffering. We make peace with suffering and receive it as a treasured part of life.

"The infinite lies stretched in smiling repose" because the infinite does not suffer over suffering. And the infinite doesn't suffer over suffering because it knows suffering as part of the fullness of God. Like everything else, suffering belongs. In a reality beyond opposites, great love and great suffering are both essential, perhaps because they function like permanently conjoined twins. One cannot exist without the other.

So through reading and conversation, I learned an intellectual understanding of intertwined love and suffering. And once again, like all mortal beings, I needed experience to make the principle real, to "make the word flesh" (John 1:14). Stella provided that experience. She was my greatest teacher on suffering.

In my last days with Stella, I suffered without shame. I didn't look away; I didn't pretend to be brave; and through my choice to be fully present, exquisite gifts arose within me. I set aside my familiar rigidity and accepted vulnerability. This drew me into the joy and sorrow of compassion. Yes, I risked a broken heart each time I asked, "Can you walk?" and other questions like it. But I saw the unspeakable value of looking beyond my need for safety. I saw the treasure of being willing to suffer—to be present, to set aside my personal comfort, and to serve whatever was most true for Stella. This experience changed me forever.

Finally, I felt a bit like my mother on that pivotal family trip to Playland. I turned the car around. I turned away from ancestral messages that said, "Vulnerability is weakness, and weakness is failure." I turned around to face the intertwined joys and sorrows embedded in great love. Turning in the so-called wrong direction was the right direction, the right thing to do. In letting go, in choosing suffering over safety, I discovered suffering is not suffering—suffering is the new joy—the joy of "obedience to love, even unto death" (Philippians 2:8).

Reflections

Head: What does the word suffering mean to you? Do you believe it is optional?

Heart: Divine Love, help me find obedience to love, only love.

Hands: Take a risk of the heart on behalf of someone you love.

REQUIEM FOR A DOG

"Spread your wings, let your spirit soar."
—Anonymous

"It's time," I told Hugh.

He rose from the computer and strode to my office, where Stella lay on the blue carpet. She greeted him, delighted to see him. She didn't get up, but was bright-eyed alert. She thumped her tail and gave her biggest grin.

Hugh asked, "Are you sure?"

I shook my head no and shuddered at my possible miscalculation. *How will we know when it's time to end our dog's life?* I wondered.

But later as she became weaker I knew, and Hugh agreed. Tomorrow was the day. Tomorrow was the day we would carry our sweet gift of a girl to the car and drive her to the vet for the last time. Hugh asked if I would come to bed and I said, "No, I will spend this last night glued to Stella."

Somehow, she managed to haul herself up on the couch, leaving just enough room for me to spoon behind her like I always did. I climbed in and draped my arm over her chest to hold onto her heartbeat. I burrowed under a blanket and watched bad television. I waited for sleep and dreaded the morning.

I slept, then a shudder awakened me. I felt Stella's body tremble. She exhaled slowly and her heart stopped.

What is this? I thought. She inhaled deeply. Then her heart fluttered, fibrillated like a tiny bird. She exhaled and it was over. Her heart stopped in my hand. I waited. There was endless silence where my dog used to be. My medical training kicked in and I said, "Time of death, 2:27." She was gone. What would I do without my North Star?

I would look for her everywhere and come up missing. I would sing my daily soundtrack of silly dog songs and realize the songs no longer applied. I would sing the songs in a minor key. I would refuse to listen to opera, especially Puccini. I would not eat an almond because Stella was not there to point and drool. I would build a shrine of worn designer dog collars, lit by Mexican Jesus and Mary candles.

I would pretend Bartie was Stella, so I could feel her again, and then hate myself when this degrading attempt didn't work. I would facilitate the animal blessing service at church and collapse by the "In Loving Memory" table—the place where people put pictures of their deceased pets. Then I would frighten the volunteers as I placed my hands over my eyes for 30 minutes of unstoppable tears.

I would limp through infinite "firsts without Stella." The first hike in the Ojai Canyons, the first dinner party, the first beach trip, the first cheese, the first everything because she was everything to me.

I would sigh and ponder the Rainbow Bridge—that tear-inducing poem about pets in heaven waiting to be reunited with their earth-bound companions. Maybe she's playing in heaven with the other dead dogs, wrestling the crap out of them. Maybe she'll be there, poised and waiting for me when I pass over. Maybe she'll greet me, and we'll cross the Rainbow Bridge together.

When I die, if there's no Rainbow Bridge, if I go to the other side and she's not there, I'll hunt down the liar who wrote that stinking poem and slap her.

In the midst of heartache, I would cling to a day in May, one month before the onset of Stella's fast, undiagnosable illness, back when things were whole.

Stella and Bartie, with Mali the cat, proudly worked as a team to bring a live hummingbird into the house. Through some miracle of grace, guidance, and animal control, I caught the bird in my hands. I held it, captivated by rapid wings beating against my palms. I felt its holy longing to be free. I brought the hummingbird outside by our hibiscus plant, opened my hands, and the bird soared upwards like a prayer.

I remember Stella's last heartbeat and how it felt like the hummingbird. Stella's heart held captive by a frail body that could no longer contain the largeness of her love; her heart that strained against captivity and transformed yearning into spaciousness; her heartbeat that flew so swiftly away, into wild grace.

Was the hummingbird a sign? I wanted it to be. I proclaimed, "Stella, I will look for you in hummingbirds. I will see each one as a messenger that tells me you are not gone, but free."

Then I sighed and whispered, "And when there are no hummingbirds, I will pray for sleep—and hope to dream of you, beside me, back home, where you belong."

Reflections:

Head: What losses have you experienced? How do you manage grief?

Heart: Divine Love, teach me my loved one is not gone, but free.

Hands: Write a love letter to someone who has passed on.

Stella Rose, July 15, 2002 - July 13, 2013.

37
TEARS AT A TEA PARTY

"Beware, this is a place for tears."
—Giacomo Puccini, Tosca

A couple of months after Stella died, I still grieved as I went through the motions of ministry. Three sweet church ladies invited me to a tea party at their retirement community. When I read the invitation, I sighed. The words "tea party" evoked a childhood memory.

My parents hoped to shape their four daughters into "little ladies." My mother had a large collection of fine teacups on display in a wooden cabinet. We used these and the Wedgewood China every night for dinner, with candles and linen napkins. My sisters and I all played instruments and gathered to make chamber music on Sunday afternoons. We took cotillion, ballroom dance lessons where we wore white gloves and learned to curtsey to the chaperones. Often in the mornings, we would read from an immense Amy Vanderbilt Book of Etiquette stashed in our breakfast nook.

We also had a lot of pets—two ducks, a series of dogs, cats, hamsters, guinea pigs, white mice, rabbits, turtles, lizards, and more. The animals in our house offered a Noah's Ark ambiance that sometimes overrode our parents' attempts at refinement.

Judy, a Horse, Nancy, Carol, and Bonnie.

One day, our dog, Jinx, scaled the kitchen table and ate a chunk out of Amy Vanderbilt's dissertation on social graces. Shortly thereafter, Jinx threw up on a placemat near the shredded remains of the book. My mother dabbed at the dog vomit with a cloth napkin while my sister, Nancy, suggested writing a letter to Amy Vanderbilt to tell her about Jinx's breach.

"She devoured the book but didn't quite digest the material," she joked.

When the church ladies invited me to the tea party, I thought about Jinx's throw up. I knew I could be polite and conversational, but I was still so sad about Stella. I dreaded sitting, sipping tea, and making conversation for hours. I thought, *Maybe if I vomit on a placemat, I can get out of it.* That didn't seem like a viable option, so I agreed to go and do my best.

The invitation said, "Bring your favorite teacup!" so I dug out our wedding China. I shaved the furry pelt off of my legs and kissed our remaining Vizsla Bartie good-bye. I entered the community's recreation room wearing a dainty dress and a forced smile. I sat at the table with three other women, revived my stoicism, and pretended to be happy.

The hostess announced there would be entertainment—a soprano from Los Angeles Opera. *Fine,* I inwardly growled. *I hope she doesn't suck.* The singer took her place in the crook of the piano. She launched into her first aria, and I became unglued. Puccini. She sang Puccini. I had banned Puccini the day Stella died.

Giacomo Puccini was a well-known opera composer. He is known for emotional (some say maudlin) music. Once I read a definition of opera that said, *"A soprano falls in love with a tenor, and then a baritone comes along and ruins everything."* That formulaic plot, or something like it, sounds like typical Puccini, but I didn't care. I loved his music.

When Stella was alive, I listened to opera whenever I cooked. While I celebrated memories of professional singing, Stella stood close beside me, mesmerized by my food prep. These moments of singing along with recorded opera in my kitchen were better than any of my live performances. I was home with my diva dog, who was riveted by the possibility that a scrap of tofu might leap off the parapet of the cutting board and bounce to the floor for her pleasure.[31]

At the tea party, the soloist sang one Puccini aria after

---

31 This is a reference to the opera *Tosca*, by Giacomo Puccini. At the end of the opera, Tosca leaps off a parapet to her death. (Sorry to spoil the ending).

another. She was a great singer. My eyes filled, and I started to cry into my teacup. Dammit, this was the price of choosing suffering over safety, the price of being present. Blubbering at a tea party.

The church ladies glanced nervously at me, probably wondering why I was having a nervous breakdown. After a few minutes, I started laughing—laughing because I was sobbing at a tea party, wiping snot with my cloth napkin, wondering: *what would Amy Vanderbilt do?* Suddenly, I was grateful for all of it.

The gentle church ladies asked, "Are you okay?"

"It's just so beautiful—that is one fantastic singer," I said as I cried. "And my dog died…and I'm still sad that my mother died 37 years ago. And I love my life…and I love you for inviting me to this tea party that made me cry."

Then there was a glut of gratitude for my whole life—the privilege of being raised in a family where we valued art and culture. But also how we could laugh at a pile of dog barf poised on the kitchen table beside an etiquette book. A childhood where I learned to do the waltz, the foxtrot, and the cha-cha like the "little lady" my parents wanted me to be. Then the laughter when the cotillion teacher asked us to remove our white gloves for punch and cookies by bellowing, "Not with your teeth girls!"

Oh, and the dearness of all of that and so much more, the bitter sweetness of a mother who died too young but taught us to value life. And now the blessings of our church family, that brought me pain at times, but also the joy of delicious tears at a tea party. I thought of every detail of my humble human existence and celebrated with Shakespeare the "tongues in trees, books in the running brooks, sermons in stones, and good in everything." And how like Shakespeare, "I would not change it," not any of it, not even Stella, or my mom.

As I left, I thanked the church ladies and the opera singer for unknowingly serving me. I was grateful for the collision of laughter and tears. I was grateful for the mystery—a strange mix of emotions that somehow brought me to an inner sanctuary, a place to reconcile stoicism and sobbing. Most of all, I was grateful for God's immaculate stagecraft—how she assembled all the players in the perfect place, at a time when I needed them most. The church ladies didn't know this, but God knew. God knew that after the tears at a tea party, I had to attend a meeting in my church office. It was to plan a funeral. There would be no fun in this funeral.

Reflections

Head: What is the price of being present to all of your feelings?

Heart: Divine Love, find me a good cry when I need it. Let my tears turn to gratitude for all seen and unseen blessings.

Hands: Move through your day with the eyes to see "good in everything."

LOVE AND LOSS

"Without a hurt, the heart is hollow."
—Tom Jones

A healthy young man died suddenly and tragically in a car accident, late at night, on a dirt road off a highway near Missoula, Montana. The young man's name was Josh. His parents live near the church, so they contacted me to do Josh's memorial. I met with them immediately after the tea party. We sat in my office, stunned, tearful, angry, and silent all at the same time. There was nothing to say, no way to comfort them. All I could do was be present. All I could do was sit with them and listen to the "sound of hearts breaking, the silent scream of unspeakable grief."[vi]

We planned the memorial as best we could, trying to do the impossible, trying to capture someone infinite and precious in a single service. Later, Josh's mother, Deana, told me she and her family traveled to Missoula shortly after her son died. They went to grieve, to learn more about Josh's death, and to cherish any reminders of his too-brief time on earth. They also wanted to build a cross to place at the crash site.

Deana, her husband, and some of Josh's friends drove to a local hardware store to purchase wood, paint, and other supplies to make the cross. At the hardware store, Deana wandered away from the others and found an aisle of wind chimes of all sizes. When she saw the chimes, she was overcome with an urgent need to make noise, to crack the sky. She staggered down the wind chime aisle and rang them all. "I was *required* to make a sound," she said. "Each bell I rang gave me more energy."

When Deana told me this story, I sat silently as I felt her grief—a grief too great for mere tears. I suddenly understood how her pain needed the truth of pealing bells, a sonnet for her beloved boy. Then I stopped breathing. I didn't want to exhale into a world of such cruel impermanence. At the same time, I wanted to inhale Deana's passion, to take in the exquisite love of a despairing mother and magnify it forever. As I listened to her, I navigated the narrow way, suspended like a wire between the fragility of love and the power of loss.

Years later, I still think of Deana when grief finds me. Through her story, and others like it, I honor the inevitable intertwining of joy and sorrow. I think about my own pain, my mother's death that hurt because we loved her so. Or Stella's last day when I bowed to love's calling and asked, "Can you walk?" I ponder why we invite dogs and other beings into our lives, when we know their mortality will someday hurt us.

Then I think about opera. Opera may be a story about a soprano, a tenor, and a ruinous baritone, but it's also a story about alchemy. Those who love opera go to the theater to cry on purpose. The plot happens, the music soars, the characters undergo great pain for the sake of love, and we mourn. Is this foolish? Is it masochistic? No, because somehow in brokenness, ecstasy and sorrow merge to generate something greater than the sum of the parts, something golden that purifies us.

Is opera life? Is life opera? Do we secretly yearn for a world that offers a ridiculous combination platter of pain and passion?

If so, what should we do about it? Should we avoid it, should we allow it, should we let it go?

I don't know the answers to these questions. Not yet. Not fully. But in the living and dying, I ask myself, as if I were my beloved Stella, "Can you walk, sweetheart? Can you walk?" It's a metaphor: Will you be present to everything? Will you trust God's brilliant design?

I say yes. For somehow, with each tentative step, I get a glimpse of what it is like to accept love *and* loss as transient parts of priceless being. When I touch the hem of this holy garment, I believe I *can* walk. Or better yet, I can fall—fall in love with a foreign homeland beyond birth and death. Fall in love with a place where laughter and tears are one—a place where I am embraced by a mother, a dog, and the echo of bells keening for a child.

Reflections

Head: What are your thoughts on love and loss?

Heart: Divine Love, help me be present to everything. Hold me as I honor both joy and sorrow.

Hands: Spend some time in nature or another place that puts you in touch with life beyond birth and death.

PART SEVEN:

FROM GRIEF TO GRATITUDE

OM SARASWATI

"May Goddess Saraswati bless your life with success, happiness, love, and warmth."
—Traditional Hindu Blessing

Is impermanence life's only permanent condition? It seems like everything transforms in the wake of linear time. Transformation is the essence of existence. This may challenge us—but we find peace in transformation as we remember the changeless grace underlying all changes. Impermanence *is* grace; it is love, hope, and happiness in disguise—for what would life be without impermanence?

The day I sobbed into my teacup, something cracked open. It was a beginning—a nascent vision of grief's capacity to morph into gratitude. Not only gratitude for life's pleasures, but also gratitude for the mixture of love and loss that brings transcendental joy.

About joy: humans can find ways to be ashamed of almost anything, even their finest qualities. I've always been embarrassed by my joy. True, sometimes it's juvenile or annoying. Sometimes I employ fake joy to smother unwanted feelings. But even when joy is irrepressible and appropriate, I think, *Why can't you be more serious like the other grownups?* I stuff my exuberance into a mental girdle. As is the case with most girdles, eventually something pops out in a strange place. Something like a naked burrito, a vet licking, or fun at funerals.

Stella, who was dog-joy incarnate, encourages me from the other side. As promised, she comes to me in hummingbirds. When hummingbirds soar into our back yard to drink the nectar of our red trumpet vine flowers, I remember Stella. Hummingbirds, Stella, and the other mystics tell me our true nature is unconditional joy. We belong to unconditional joy as unconditional joy belongs to us.

About a year after Stella died, I attended a workshop with renowned author and healer, Rachel Naomi Remen. The workshop was for doctors, nurses, and clergy. The intent was to help us find our larger spiritual purpose within the context of work. Every time we contemplated the question of purpose, through lectures, conversations, or meditations, I kept hearing, "Bonnie, joy is your purpose. Deal with it."

We went on a break, and I walked through the neighborhood. As I walked, I reflected on the rowdy joy that seems to possess me at times. I wondered if joy was an appropriate purpose. My delight in human clumsiness. My fascination with telling disgusting nursing stories about bodily mishaps. Or the time I charmed two Japanese teenagers in India because I knew how to say "fart" in their native tongue. (I learned the word from a Japanese cast member during the *Lettice and Lovage* tour and I never forgot.)[32] Again, I thought, *Shouldn't you just grow up, Bonnie? Shouldn't you get serious about the pain, pestilence, and suffering in the world?*

In the midst of this reverie about shame and joy, I turned a corner and saw a Vizsla puppy leaping and rolling on her front lawn. She was about six months old. I asked the pet parents if I could play with her. They said yes, so I laid on the grass and let the

---

32 Fart in Japanese is Onora – pronounced oh-no-RAH.

puppy crawl all over me. When I finally tore myself away to return to my seminar, it felt like Stella had again sent me a customized message. The message was, *"I placed a perfectly timed baby Vizsla to awaken you to your natural destiny. Devote yourself to joy. Be the riotous delight that infuses puppies, children, flowers, the stars, the moon, the sun, human mishaps, and Japanese farts—this is your meaning and purpose. Let your joy shine everywhere."*

Then there were the healers. One hypnotherapist offered me a life-between-life hypnosis experience. He showed me how Stella's joy has been with me through many lifetimes. Under hypnosis, when I left one life to cross over to another, Stella was there to greet me, to jump up and lick my face. I remembered how I questioned the existence of the Rainbow Bridge after Stella died. How I said I would slap the author of the Rainbow Bridge poem if the bridge didn't exist. In my life between life experience, there was no Rainbow Bridge. A bridge would have been too small. There was a rainbow acre filled with hundreds of pets—loved, lost, and found again—animals from many incarnations. This affirmed more joy, beyond the physical.

I visited another well-known animal communicator shortly after Stella died. I wanted to connect with Stella, to discern what she was feeling in her last days and where she was now. This psychic affirmed our shared joy, and at the very end of our session, she said Stella would communicate with me from the other side through the wind.

After much grief and gratitude, Hugh and I decided to open our hearts to another Vizsla. I found a breeder, made plans, and loaded Bartie in the car to drive up to Northern California to greet the new puppy. As I pulled onto the freeway, I saw a huge billboard that said "Stella Rosa." It's a wine, but the timing of the signage felt like another joy-memo from our Stella Rose. When I arrived at the breeder's house after a six-hour drive, I got out of the car and a gust of wind almost knocked me over. "Stella will communicate with you through the wind," the psychic said.

We adopted baby Saraswati and called her Sara for short. Her name was a tribute to my journey in India, where I carried Stella in my heart. Saraswati is a Hindu Goddess but was also the name of my favorite security guard in the hotel where we briefly stayed before heading to the ashram. Saraswati the security guard checked us daily for hidden weapons. She patted us down gently and reverently pawed through my purse. In a time when I was hurting, aching for my dying dog, I cherished her kindness.

When we got Saraswati the puppy, I took her out for her first tinkle near the hotel where we stayed in an ultra-conservative Christian northern California town. I rounded a corner and saw a Hindu temple, another sign from Stella. She nudged me with her consent from beyond the veil. "You are doing the right thing by getting this puppy," she said. "Always invite more joy."

Sara came home, and the playful menace of a new puppy began. There were months of potty training. Months of her scampering through the house like a John Deere thresher, looking for something to shred. We went to dog training classes for both Sara and Bartie, because Bartie regressed in the presence of a puppy. Both of them wrestled and chased each other throughout the house, sometimes tangling with Mali our cat, and often capsizing lamps, knickknacks, and small pieces of furniture. Somehow in the ruckus, I rediscovered enduring wholeness and reset my inner compass toward reverence for heavenly disorder—and I learned to cherish grace, humbly disguised as boisterous joy.

Woody Allen tells this story in the movie Annie Hall: "Two elderly women are at a Catskill Mountain resort, and one of them says, 'Boy, the food at this place is really terrible.' The other one says, 'Yeah, I know; and such small portions.' Well, that's essentially how I feel about life—full of loneliness, and misery, and suffering, and unhappiness, and it's all over much too quickly."

Yes. Signs and wonders from Stella, our dearly departed dog. Then Saraswati, our new little Vizsla goddess who helped transmute the darkness of loss into light. Hugh, Bartie, the other animals, and me, all of us, dancing through chaos; laughing at the continuum of exuberant being now in a new rusty fur coat; and trusting somehow it all makes sense. This joy, this reckless grace, this is living. Unbridled, undying living. And "it's all over much too quickly" —yet it's somehow eternal, too.

Sara chewed a hole in my pants so I put them on her head.

Reflections

Head: Do you have a word of purpose? Are you confident in your purpose?

Heart: Divine Love, teach me to celebrate my holy purpose in all that is given.

Hands: Engage in an activity that honors your word of purpose. Give your purpose time and space to thrive. Love your purpose and allow your purpose to love you.

THE SOUND OF WINGS

"God is love, lover, and beloved."
—Sufi saying

A friend and I often greet each other with the Arabic words, "Ishq Allah." Ishq is passionate love for God. Crazy love for spirit in matter and matter in spirit. The Sufi-dervish-wonder that whirls and says, *Ishq Allah ma'būd lillāh, God is love, lover, and beloved.*[33]

Sara and Bartie hike with me in the mountains where Sara brings a special brand of Ishq. Whenever she senses a bird, she freezes in a perfect point. Time stops as she leans forward, her front leg bent, her stubby tail extended. It's dog yoga, downward pointing God, as she claims union with her ordained purpose.

I hold my breath. The earth holds its breath.

Then Sara hears a sacred starting gun, discernible only in dog-land. She barrels into the underbrush. Twenty grey quail fling themselves up out of the bushes, no chirping, only the sound of insistent wings that say, "I Am." I inhale the sound of wings and say, "So Am I, beloved quail—I Am." Sara barks at the quail then races back down the mountain to share her excitement with Bartie

---
[33] Pronounced eeshk allah mahbood leelah. Translation by Hazrat Inayat Khan.

and me. "You are the beloved, too, sweet dogs," I say. Together, we continue our ishq-intoxicated hike.

What did I do to deserve this microcosm of audacious grace? Who created a dog that points so clearly and dearly? What offers a flock of quail the adventure of a shared get-away? How do air, feathers, and flight conspire to break one's heart into beauty with sounds only love can hear? Who submits us to this drunken recklessness?

Ishq allāh ma'būd lillāh, God as love, lover, and beloved…

What a privilege it is to listen to the three in one. No definitions, no reasoning required. Simply wonder in the wordless wings.

Love, lover, and beloved sing to us constantly. But will we listen? Will we hear?

With love's help, I'll try and listen better. I'll start with the high school band that rehearses every day, inches from my house. I'll fall in love with their raucous *On Wisconsin*. I'll shimmy to the salsa version of Beethoven's *Für Elise*. I'll dance to the drum line. I'll trust love to transform out-of-tune band music to the sound of teenagers pointing their clarinets and saxophones toward the intangible angle of grace. I'll know the music hasn't changed. The beloved changes *me*. The lover tempts my ears to hear differently. And the alchemy of love transforms annoyance into amazement.

With practice, we can learn everything is love, lover, and beloved. Dissonance and grace; the New York Philharmonic and the Santa Paula High School band—It's all the sound of wings. It's all *Ishq Allāh ma'būd lillāh*. Everything is intoxicated rapture calling us home—home to heaven on earth, precisely, where we belong.

Reflections

Head: Where can you apply the realization of love, lover, and beloved?

Prayer: Divine Love, infuse my life with your audacious grace.

Hands: Stay alert to whatever is "out of tune" in your life. Then pray to transform annoyance to amazement.

41

THE WHOLE WORLD IS ONE FAMILY

"This is mine, that is his, say the small minded; The wise believe that the entire world is a family."
—Maha Upanishad 6.71–75

Stella died at 2:27 a.m. on a Saturday. Twelve-and-a-half hours later, I was scheduled to pick up Nipun at the airport for another evening event at our church. Several volunteers offered to fetch him for me, but I said no. I wanted to stop crying and do something constructive. I needed a task. Plus, I knew Nipun's presence would be soothing.

Hugh and I drove from Santa Paula to Burbank Airport. As we barreled down a speedy Los Angeles freeway, a small black sedan ahead of us struck an obstacle in the road and spun out of control. It made several 360-degree turns across all four southbound lanes and landed on the median. I watched it in slow motion. Part of me thought, *Is this it? Are we coming to meet you on the other side, Stella?* Despite my grief, I knew I wasn't ready. I wanted to live.

All of the drivers, including Hugh, stepped on their brakes and engaged in an almost choreographed swerve and slow down. Everyone went exactly where they needed to go. No one crashed and no one was hurt. In a city where traffic accidents happen every day, it was a miracle. Was this divine intervention? Did a new guardian angel arrive in the afterlife at 2:27 a.m.? Did this angel have a red coat and floppy ears? Stella was hypervigilant on behalf of her loved ones when she was in her physical body. Perhaps she watched us from the other side. When she saw the potential wreckage, she barked at reality and said, "Not yet!" Maybe because she wanted me to be around for what was to happen next.

In the coming years, our church continued to thrive as a center of love. We built a strong community that brought small, yet mighty acts of kindness to the world. When cancel culture became a cause for many, we leaned into compassion culture. We saw compassion as a meeting place for love and appropriate boundaries. Love plus integrity provides a space for redemption, a place where victims are empowered, and at least the possibility of reconciliation, where a perpetrator can summon true remorse.

Our church strives to create an environment where all are welcome regardless of race, sexual orientation, class, political affiliations, religion, skill set, or status. We do our best to look past the socially constructed ideas that so many use as excuses for rage and division. Like Superman, we use our X-ray vision, our values, to look through self-imposed walls and see the truth of oneness that connects all of us.

We cultivate grace and forgiveness. We allow mistakes and try our best to celebrate them as a path of awakening. Our mistakes teach us. They belong as part of the comical, human, divine condition. From a non-dual cosmic view, mistakes are never mistakes. They are, among other things, opportunities to laugh and to learn the humble art of apology.

Over the years, my friendship with Nipun and ServiceSpace grew. I visited northern California several times to attend

ServiceSpace gatherings. I met Nipun's family and attended several meditation circles held in Nipun's parents' home.

Nipun's mother and father, Harshida and Dinesh, started a meditation practice many years ago with a few eager participants. The circle grew and now they host 60-plus people every week. We sit elbow-to-elbow in a modest living room. The crowd overflows into the dining room and foyer. We meditate in silence for an hour. Then we share reflections about a sacred reading for another hour. Afterwards, we dine in silence. Harshida and several volunteers prepare a home-cooked vegetarian meal for all the participants. The practice has become global, as people all over the world host their own versions of this practice, now called Awakin' Circles, to awaken with kin.

When I attended the Awakin' Circles in northern California, I noticed how Harshida serves quietly behind-the-scenes with a gracious spirit and spacious heart. One time during a group share, she spoke about her beloved vegetable garden. She borrows vegetables from the garden to feed her guests. She said, "I always leave some zucchini for the squirrels." Another time, I asked Harshida where to shop for Indian clothes in their neighborhood. She bustled over to her closet and started giving me *her* clothes.

Then one day I learned about Harshida's response to Nipun's pilgrimage. As I mentioned before, Nipun and his wife, Guri, sold their possessions, left safety and comfort behind, and walked across India.

I wasn't there when the newly married, 20-something Nipun told his mother of his intentions, but I like to imagine the conversation went something like this:

"Um, Mom, Guri and I are going to India."

"Wonderful, my son! Where are you staying?"

"Well mom, see that's the thing. We're walking 600 miles without any money. We're going to rely on the kindness of strangers. We'll eat whatever food is offered, sleep where we can, and trust that love will provide."

After a pause… "Excuse me?"

"Now mom, don't worry."

"But I need to know where you are. Do you have a roadmap… an itinerary?"

"Yes, mom…um…we'll be guided by a heart of service."

"How will I get in touch with you?"

"Well, you won't be able to…but I'll only go with your blessing."

"I can't let you go."

I feel Harshida's anguish. I'm not a mother of humans, but I did "pull a Broadway Tour out of the ethers" so I could be with my cat. I pine for our dogs, our rabbit, our cat, and our guinea pigs if I stay overnight in a luxury hotel in an adjacent county. Nipun asked his mother for something near impossible. Harshida was supposed to not only allow her son to embark upon a potentially dangerous journey—she was supposed to bless it.

A mother embodies the need to care at all costs. A mother is called to nurture, even to risk her own life for the well-being of a beloved child. The call to care is embedded in a mother's physiology. It's why a mother can lift a car to save a baby or how she can go without food so her child can eat.

Nipun asked Harshida to release generations of genetic programming and social conditioning. He asked her to transcend her hormones, DNA, and muscle memory to support his journey. He asked her to surrender her heart to appalling uncertainty. He gave her the grueling task of leaning on faith in the face of severe doubt. How could she possible say yes? How could she let go of her beloved son?

Nipun and his mother had many more conversations about this journey. Then one day, Nipun said, "Mom, you'll stay here, but you'll also go on this pilgrimage with me." Harshida looked at him, puzzled.

Nipun reminded his mother of how she raised him with the principle of "Vasudhaiva Kutumbakam," a Sanskrit phrase meaning "the whole world is one family." Then he told Harshida, "If you ever worry about your son being hungry, feed someone here knowing it will nourish me on the other side of the planet. If you feel like your son doesn't have a place to stay, house someone. If you worry I'm not safe, offer safety to another. You've always taught me when we commit to a pilgrim's heart, boundaries start to dissolve, gratitude and reverence awaken, and the gentle whispers of our service inexplicably tilt the world toward greater love."

He paused and asked, "Mom, will you go on this pilgrimage with me?"

With tears in her eyes, Harshida looked at her son and said, "Yes, I will make this pilgrimage with you. And I will give you my blessing."

While Nipun and Guri walked through India, Harshida offered small acts of service to friends and strangers. Her actions may have been barely noticeable to many, like Nipun's great-grandfather feeding the ants in India. But these small offerings undoubtedly changed hearts around the globe. In fact, Harshida's actions change hearts even today as we share this story together and consider her noble sacrifice.

Sacrifice means to make something sacred. Much is lost, yet more is gained through the sacred art of letting go. The choice to love without limits asks us to sacrifice ordinary love for mystical love. Mystical love stretches us past the practical, the rational, and the normal. It asks us to grow into grace beyond human understanding.

I contemplate Harshida's blessed sacrifice and ask again,

How do we know when to hold on and when to let go? Is it possible letting go gives us the soul-happiness that we crave? If so, how do we navigate this process our egos barely understand?

The only discernment tool that comes to me is this: some truths are too truthful to ignore. Resting in the principle of "the whole world is one family" allows us to shift our thinking, even as we continue to doubt. Somehow, we know through conscience and intuition, a mystical presence longs to shine through our release.

Then we back up our shift in thinking with action: "acting as if" the whole world is our family, caring for strangers, feeding the hungry, committing ourselves to actions that make the principle real. We bridge the gap from the profound to the practical and back again. We live like the truth is true. We tear ourselves from routine, rational modes of being. We renounce safety and leap into a void of uncertainty that offers paradoxical comfort.

In the uncertainty, the magic grows. We hold without holding on. We explore divine territory in our frail yet mighty human hearts. We lean into the mystical marriage of uncertainty and trust. We see how uncertainty and trust bless and amplify one another. And if we're willing to stay in the vague discomfort of unknowing, our hearts twist into a strange inner loop, a double helix, a new DNA where greatness can emerge—not greatness as the world knows it, but greatness of the soul.

Do we dare take the risk? Do we dare to plunge headfirst into the unknown, to dive into deep water without our normal lifeguards on standby?

Perhaps instead of plunging headfirst, we plunge heart first. We plunge into a visceral knowing of the divine connection between all beings. We trust that helping a hungry person in Northern California feeds a hungry son in India. We learn to believe as we swim in this pool of amplified oneness, and everything becomes a blessing. Our intentions, actions, results, and ripples overflow to benefit the cosmos.

Nipun returned safely home, changed for good because of the pilgrimage. Once he was back, he admitted to Harshida her pilgrimage had been much harder than his. Yes, he walked in 120-degree heat and at times lacked food or shelter. But he and Guri went voluntarily. They went on purpose with a sense of excitement. Harshida sacrificed the dearest thing in the world. She let go, dove in heart first, and her willingness changed everything.

Just like she taught Nipun, her sacrifice "inexplicably tilted the world toward greater love."

Guri and Nipun Mehta, pilgrimage across India.

Reflections

Head: What does the principle of "the whole world is one family" mean to you?

Heart: Divine Love, help me see the whole world as one family.

Hands: Live like the truth is true. Serve a local stranger on behalf of a distant loved one.

42

THEN IS NOW, AND THERE IS HERE

"If you as a human being transform yourself, you affect the consciousness of the rest of the world."

—Krishnamurti

The idea of "Vasudhaiva Kutumbakam—the whole world is one family" shows up in the New Testament. In the book of Matthew Jesus speaks to his listeners and says, "For I was hungry, and you gave me something to eat, I was thirsty, and you gave me something to drink, I was a stranger and you invited me in, I needed clothes, and you clothed me, I was sick, and you looked after me, I was in prison, and you came to visit me."

Jesus's audience said, "Jesus! When did we see you hungry and feed you, or thirsty and give you something to drink? When did we see you as a stranger and invite you in, or clothe you? When did we see you sick or in prison and go to visit you?"

Jesus replies, "Truly I tell you, whatever you did for one of the least of these brothers and sisters of mine, you did for me" (Matthew 25: 35-40).

From a metaphorical standpoint, this story sheds light on an ongoing tug-of-war between ego and mystical awareness.

Jesus's audience was confused, even though they sincerely tried to understand him. This chorus of confusion operates from ego. The ego takes Jesus's words literally. The separate self sees people as separate beings. It relies on linear logic and asks, "How can kindness to a distant, other person possibly provide kindness to you, Jesus? How can kindness to one of us offer kindness to all of us? It makes no sense whatsoever!"

This gospel message addresses the doubts we may experience when we hear small acts of kindness make an impact; or when we're invited to feed a random hungry person to alleviate the hunger of a faraway loved one. The sweet, human, separate self believes changing the world requires big gestures; and helping another requires direct contact. If our efforts don't create instant, visible results, we experience a sense of futility. So the ego postpones the work of transformation, putting it off for later, for when the place or the time is right. Or we say, "I can't do everything, so I won't do anything." This provides fertile ground for futility—helplessness and despair.

Succumbing to futility is logical according to the ego. But we can choose to disempower futility. The mere *perception* of futility, if we notice it, can move us toward sacred surrender. Through surrender, we relinquish control—the need to "fix" the world according to our anxiety-ridden ego-strategies. In the consciousness of faith-beyond-futility, a consciousness that transcends time and space, we ask: "How may I serve?"

These words harness the wholeness of the cosmos. Mystical guidance steps in to transform despair into service and helplessness into help-fullness. The awareness of ripening possibilities awakens within us. This awakening springs to life to affirm the expansive power of what we *can* do. We rely on the confidence of our eternal interconnection. And we trust the whole world is not only our family—it is *us*.

I am you and you are me. We are the I Am presence, the oneness anointed by love, simply because we exist as part of the whole. We are the divine having a human experience—immediately here, and now in all things.

When we immerse ourselves in this reality, we regain hope. We know changing ourselves changes the world. We trust feeding one person begins to feed all of us. We know offering shelter, shelters God. We no longer *delay* our desire to serve the whole world. We release *waiting for the right time and place* and we embrace absolute reality in the moment. We embody a consciousness where *then is now* and *there is here*.

If this is confusing, don't worry. It is not meant to be understood by the binary brain, only trusted and lived. Spiritual truth calls us to peel away the tenacious logic of the ego and embody a new affirmative reality. Truth calls us to act from an awareness of oneness, always.

Do you long to be part of an ever-expanding circle of blessedness? Are you willing to trust a reality where blessing anything blesses everything? Will you expand your circle of love by blessing yourself and blessing others? Will you reveal how the world is transformed by *you*, by each of us, doing what we can where we are, one benevolent gesture at a time?

If so, trust that small acts of service matter. See the world, not as broken, but evolving. Nurture hope and inspiration. And kneel before love's spaciousness, to serve the whole world simply, with joy.

Reflections

Head: Where do you succumb to futility, helplessness, or despair?

Heart: Divine Love, help me leap past logic and trust that serving one of us serves all of us.

Hands: Serve another being and abide in the awareness of serving the whole world.

PART EIGHT:

GLOBAL KINDNESS

BACK TO INDIA

"Everything in the world was my guru."
—Ramana Maharshi

In January of 2018, I boarded a plane back to India. There was no dying dog at home this time, but still I felt like I was flying into a mystery. ServiceSpace summoned me to a gathering called Gandhi 3.0. When people asked me why I was going, again I said, "I don't know." When they asked for more information I said, "I think it's a meeting of humanitarian leaders from all over the world, in Ahmedabad, near the Gandhi Ashram. I suppose we'll meditate and such." All I knew was Nipun invited me, and my answer was an immediate yes. Once again, I was called to know nothing and trust everything.

I arrived at the airport in Ahmedabad in the middle of the night. The driver met me and two other Gandhi 3.0 travelers. One was an Oprah-level best-selling author, and the other was his wife, a healer. We loaded our suitcases and climbed into the van. Immediately we began a conversation about the wise fool, Nasrudin.

Nasrudin is a legendary character, central to Middle Eastern folklore. Our driver told this story: Mullah Nasrudin knelt to pray in the mosque. He became tired, so he sat on his bottom, leaned back, and rested his feet on the altar. Just then the cleric walked in and saw Nasrudin.

"How dare you!" the cleric shouted. "Remove your feet from the altar immediately, you disrespectful fool! You should never allow your feet to touch such a sacred place!"

In response, Nasrudin removed his feet, then sat with them poised in the air as he looked around for a spot to rest them. Puzzled, he responded, "If I am not permitted to rest my feet on a sacred place, then where shall I put them?"

The implication, of course, is everything is sacred. We stand on holy ground, always. This teaching story was a template for my time in India. Everything was holy ground. Every being I met was holy.

In India, we learned, sang, conversed, and danced with amazing leaders. A playful Nobel laureate made me laugh so hard, I had to sit down in the street. A renunciate—a holy man who wandered Southeast Asia with only a white cloth garment, a staff, and a pair of sandals—let me take a selfie with him after peeling vegetables together in the kitchen. I encountered volunteers who wrenched my dirty dinner dishes out of my hands, insisting they wash them for me. I met authors, actors, spiritual leaders, teachers, compassionate businesspeople, and uncommon common people—all intentional stewards of kindness.

We rode in a rickshaw with a driver who didn't charge a set fee. Rather, he asked people to "pay it forward." He trusts in generosity and his trust sends ripples of goodness into the world. We attended a kite festival, a city-wide party, where my new friends and I climbed from roof to roof to dance to Bollywood hits with welcoming strangers. We visited shrines, temples, and mosques. We meditated at the Gandhi Ashram and communed with children who washed our hands and served us dinner. Like

Nasrudin, we had no place to put our feet. We became groundless as we saw holy ground everywhere.

Sometimes in church, I do an object lesson with water and cranberry juice. I hold up a beaker of dark red unfiltered cranberry juice and say, "Imagine this is God." Then I hold up a glass of clear water and say, "Imagine this is humanity, the world, or you. We think the two are separate—that we are 'here' in the clear water, and God is 'there' in the 'good stuff,' the cranberry juice."

Young Women in Sarees, near the Gandhi Ashram.

Then I pour the cranberry juice into the water and say, "This is a more accurate model of our relationship with the divine. God infuses every atom of our being. You can't separate the water from the cranberry juice or the cranberry juice from the water. You can't separate the human from the divine. You can't separate God from God. God is a permanent part of our lives—always has been, always will be, no matter what."

India amplified this lesson about oneness. We were clear water, interwoven with the deep red nectar of love. What a blessing it was to exist in the absolute and remember the whole world is "in-formed" love. And then to ask, "What is my part to play in magnifying and multiplying this love? How can I 'in-form' love for myself and others?"

Reflections

Head: Contemplate the idea of "holy ground." Expand it to include "holy air, holy breath, holy feet, holy others." Is there anything you name unholy in your existence?

Heart: Divine Love, help me to know I always stand on holy ground.

Hands: Take a slow, contemplative walk and become conscious of your holy feet touching holy ground. "In-form" every step with deep love.

SILENT BOWS

"Wisdom tells me I am nothing. Love tells me I am everything. And between the two my life flows."
—Nisargadatta Maharaj

In India, we stayed at a retreat center developed by a local changemaker named Ishwar Patel. He passed away in 2010. A local retreat volunteer named Meghna told me about him.

When Ishwar was in fifth grade, his teacher asked the students to participate in a cleaning competition. Ishwar swept the nearby streets with a broom. As he was sweeping, a woman walked by and exclaimed, "This broom is a tool of an untouchable!" She found a vessel of water, dipped her gold earring in it, then splashed the water on Ishwar's face. "There," she said. "You are clean now. Don't touch a broom again."

This incident troubled Ishwar and caused him to wonder: *"Every single person creates trash, but only one type of caste picks it up. Those who throw out trash are respected in society. But those who pick trash up are treated as less than human."*[34]

The work traditionally done only by "untouchables" consisted of one human being gathering another person's waste from a dry

---

34 Based on the website: Our Roots | Environmental Sanitation Institute | Gujarat (esigujarat.org).

latrine. With bare hands, he or she placed it into a leaking bucket and carried it on their head to dispose of it outside the village. Because of this work, human scavengers were treated as the lowest of the low.

Ishwar Patel combined principles of peacemaking and science, and quietly labored to improve conditions for everyone by designing and building more than 200,000 toilets. In addition, he helped launch more than 118 organizations that would elevate the work of sanitation around the country. "To build toilets is easy," he said. "But to shift people's minds and hearts is the real work. Software is more important than hardware."[35]

Yes, it is challenging to shift minds and hearts. The woman who chastised Ishwar Patel believed in untouchables. She believed touching the broom of an untouchable could contaminate someone. She believed gold-purified water thrown in the face could undo the stain of unworthiness. She was not alone in her beliefs. Many people supported these made-up ideas. They were no more than imaginary social constructs, but they *seemed* real to those who accepted them as truth.

To change minds and hearts can seem daunting in the face of collective fear and disdain. Ishwar Patel's work was remarkable in that he didn't allow bigotry to discourage him. Instead he called forth heaven on earth by designing lowly toilets and complex sanitation systems, proving inspiration can work through anything.

Love stretches us every day, always expanding our capacity to allow the divine to serve through whatever is happening now. With consistent practice, we gain skill in seeing through the places where love seems absent. We mature spiritually; and the perceived *absence* of love becomes the willingness to reveal the

---

[35] Based on the website: Life and Death of Ishwar Patel |www.ServiceSpace.org/blog/.

concealed *presence* of love. Love is everywhere—we just need to believe it to see it.

I learned more about untouchables on my second day at the retreat. I walked with Nipun down a brick path at the center. He paused and said, "See that man over there making brooms?"

I saw an elderly gentleman with grey hair and kind eyes. He was dressed in white, sitting with other craftsmen. He was slightly stooped, yet he worked confidently and methodically. There was a stillness to him that seemed to saturate the brooms he crafted.

I nodded, and said, "Yes, who is he?"

"He lived in the slums for years," Nipun replied. "His home was a public toilet."

During my first trip to India, I used a public toilet in the slums. I walked in barefoot, and a week later my big toenail turned blue and fell off. I imagined trying to live in a public toilet and felt my body tense as I inhaled quickly.

"What's his name," I asked.

"Kanchan Mama," Nipun said. "'Mama' is like 'uncle' in India."

I watched this man work. There was something sacred about him. I remembered the part of the gospel where Jesus says, "The first shall be last, and the last shall be first" (Matthew 19:30). I saw myself in comparison, a privileged girl from the suburbs, and thought: Could I ever endure living in a latrine? Did I have even an ounce of the dignity and resilience so evident in Kanchan Mama?

"I want to meet him," I said. "Will you translate for me? Is there a way I can show my respect?"

"Touch his feet," Nipun said.

"Show me how," I replied.

Nipun brought me over to Kanchan Mama. He knelt, bowed his head, and briefly touched the elder's feet. Then he introduced me, and I did the same. With Nipun's translation, I said something inadequate, like, "You are magnificent. I have tremendous respect for you. You inspire me, and I love your brooms." It wasn't enough. Although bowing to his feet seemed to help.

Because I'm an over-zealous American, I decided to go on a bowing, foot-touching rampage. I bowed to the feet of a woman shopkeeper who gave me free wind chimes. I bowed to Jayesh, the son of Ishwar Patel, after an endearing conversation about his friendly yellow Labrador retriever. I bowed to a volunteer named Parag, just because. Oddly, all of these people leapt away or tried to touch my feet in response.

Nipun eventually took me aside and gently said, "We tend to reserve the act of bowing to the feet for our elders."

"Because they're too old to run away?" I asked.

Nipun laughed and I got the point. I switched to invisible bows—and honestly, bowing silently felt just as good. I learned another paradox: reverence for another leads to quiet exultation. Bowing elevates us.

Years later, I still think about Kanchan Mama. He was someone who was once called untouchable, or unworthy. Yet he was a spiritual teacher for me. When I watched him make brooms and learned about his past, I began to question the places and people I have named unholy. Where have I accepted disdainful and fear-based relative opinions as absolute truths?

If we're not conscious, if we don't challenge our personal truths, we use falsehoods to substantiate illusions of separation. We use random ideas like skin color, status, skill, or sexual orientation to determine acceptability. We are quick to "caste" out someone who holds different political or religious views. And then there are parts of ourselves—parts we deem shameful or untouchable.

If ever there was a time for God to roll her eyes, it would

be about this. Underneath our tirades and tantrums about worthy versus unworthy, God has already affirmed our innate holiness. Love abides in all beings. So let us bow to the world as we walk beside each other in a paradoxical mixture of humility and exultation. Let us bow and rise up as we celebrate the divine worthiness in all of us. Let us wonder at the one who dwells in every aspect of our lives. Let us remember there is nothing within us love cannot transform.

Spinning at the Gandhi Ashram.

Reflections

Head: What feels untouchable in your life? Where did you learn this story? Do you believe it?

Heart: Divine Love, reveal the parts of myself that feel shameful or untouchable. Heal me and help me forgive, breathe, and bow inwardly.

Hands: Spend a day secretly bowing to those around you. Notice how bowing elevates the soul.

UNCONDITIONAL SUCCESS

"When we give ourselves permission to fail, we, at the same time, give ourselves permission to excel."
—Eloise Ristad

"I am no longer ashamed of my shame." I said that affirmation years ago when I first started addressing my challenges in ministry. Shame felt like the untouchable part of me. What was I ashamed of? Well everything, but mostly failure.

I was ashamed to fail as are most of us. We attack ourselves for failing even if we fail in private, even if we allegedly fail in the context of our own inner monologues regarding what we think we've done wrong. Private failure feels bad. But failing in public is a whole other matter. The sting of failure is magnified when everyone knows about it. Failure leads to perceived untouchability as we feel cast out from the good opinions of others.

You may remember I had a long, tangled relationship with failure. God had something to teach me about it: how failure is an illusion of the ego, how failure gains power through relentless self-flogging. Love schooled me in the ways of public failure by thrusting me into one career after another where I could fail big in front of a lot of people. That's why this sensitive introvert chose to act, sing, work as a corporate trainer, and then become a minister. These were all prime opportunities for public humiliation.

As I mentioned before, ministry taught me to disempower failure by befriending it. I learned everyone fails, and we don't need to take failure personally. It's part of a bigger picture of wholeness. Yet, I still felt a smidgen or perhaps a boatload of attachment around impressing others. I still wanted people to like me, maybe even think I was special.

When I went to India with a vision to serve, I *thought* I should be past the need for approval. However, I noticed the God in India *and* the God in the United States both enjoyed capsizing my ego. I guess there really is only one God embracing all religions, peoples, and lands—and the one God found me, again, in India. God wanted me to learn more, to nudge me to a place where I could say with a Yogananda paraphrase, "I am not afraid of failure; failure is afraid of me." The only way I could believe these words and *mean* them was to challenge the illusion of failure. I had to flop in public and then move into the joy of the divine—a joy so vast and inclusive it enfolds failure. Yuck.

Love planted seeds for failure during a car ride through the city of Ahmedabad. Thank God I was a passenger, because driving in India is, let's say, different than driving in the United States. I remember one time our driver zipped through a stop sign. I casually asked, "Wow, aren't you afraid you'll get a ticket?" He replied, "Here in India, a stop sign is just a suggestion."

Many of the streets are narrow and cobbled. People drive fast in many different kinds of vehicles, such as motorcycles, rickshaws, cars, busses, trucks, and bicycles. There are traffic lanes, but like the stop signs, the lanes seem to be "just a suggestion." It's beautiful to watch—a proliferation of trucks painted with flowers, women in bright saris flitting through the streets like butterflies on the backs of motorcycles. Then there are the cows. They are everywhere—on the streets, in shopping malls, ambling through a crosswalk. Traffic is likely to come to an abrupt halt if a cow has a notion to cross the street. It's one of the many things I like about India.

Cows in India.

One day we were lurching around on our way to a restaurant, and I started to sing one of my roller coaster songs. A voice teacher once told me I should never ever scream because unsupported screaming could irritate one's vocal cords. So I sang opera arias on roller coasters and such.

Usually I sang the *Salve Regina* from *The Dialogues of the Carmelites*—an opera about nuns during the French Revolution. It's not a cheery opera. Spoiler alert: it ends with all but one of the Carmelite nuns getting their heads chopped off. The nuns sing the *Salve* as they approach the guillotine. They pray to the blessed Virgin Mary for mercy. So *Salve Regina* is a good song to sing when you feel like you might die. Hence, it is appropriate for the long steep pre-drop climb on a roller coaster—or for driving in India.

I sang the *Salve* for my traveling companions in the back seat of a rickshaw. I laughed and sang through gritted teeth. The driver turned around (while driving) and said, "You're Julie Andrews!" I assured him and my fellow passengers that if anything, I was a very old and rusty Julie Andrews. But the word got out and people kept asking me to sing.

Prior to my trip to India, I said to myself, *While you're there, Bonnie, say yes to everything.* So I got my vocal cords out of the crypt and sang here and there, wherever it was helpful in some way. Our last night in India was a community night, a night when we invited many honored guests to share the blessings of the retreat. Nipun asked me to sing a few duets with a singer/guitarist from Canada, and I said yes. In a fit of false bravado masquerading as kindness, I told the guitarist, "I can learn anything. Just pick some songs and I'll be ready by tonight."

I didn't have much time to begin with. Then a cow stepped on my friend's foot and caused a slight injury. Then someone else drank the water and had a touch of intestinal distress. People knew I was a former nurse, so they asked me for advice. I did the best I could with my now-limited medical knowledge. Then I went to my room and learned my songs for the evening gathering.

I *thought* I learned my songs. When I got up to sing, I discovered I couldn't remember the melodies. I also had forgotten my reading glasses, so I couldn't see the lyrics. There was only a foggy abyss in my brain where the words and music used to live, and I didn't know what to do.

So I explained my situation to the audience. The guitarist shared his own gentle version of my story, saying, "Bonnie was generous enough to let me select our repertoire for this evening." He then carried the load of the performance, and I chimed in when I could. Sometimes I was singing in tongues, but it didn't matter. Everyone was watching me, but this was different. There was none of the accusation or judgment I associated with public failure. They watched with a sense of shared adventure, as if to say, "How wonderful! What will she do next?" They laughed, but not at me. They laughed with me as I laughed at myself.

I look back on that experience in the context of my life as a singer. When we watch an opera, there is a sometimes-snooty element of, "Can this person actually sing this aria? Will he or she crack on the high note, or will it be sublime?" On the opera stage, the performers have similar thoughts about themselves. That's what makes it exciting.

And yes, I am a fan of preparation. "God loves a prepared consciousness," one of my mentor ministers used to say. But the times when we fail—perhaps when service to a greater good impedes preparation—it's kind and wise to remember the heavens await with interest wondering, *What will she do next? Will she judge herself, or will she redefine not only failure, but success? What if her alleged failure is a fantastic lesson for herself and others? What if she is successful in a new way, a holy way that lightens the burden of perfectionism that all the dearly innocent humans impose upon themselves?*

That's how I imagine love's perception. God laughs at the language of opposites. God doesn't measure or judge. God is outrageous wholeness. In the kingdom of heaven on earth, failure and success are one.

When I remember the truth, my new definition of failure is joy. My new definition of success is joy. My new definition of everything is joy. For when I am joyful, truly joyful, I am Mullah Nasrudin, standing on holy ground—and everything flows from that awareness.

Reflections

Head: What burdens of perfectionism do you impose upon yourself? How might you alleviate these burdens? Is it possible to find comedy in failure?

Heart: Divine Love, teach me that everything provides an opportunity for humility and joy.

Hands: Learn a new skill. Treat yourself with compassion as you fail before you excel.

BUDDHISTS GONE WILD

"I slept and dreamt that life was joy. I awoke and saw that life was service. I acted and behold, service was joy."
—Rabindranath Tagore

About a year after I returned from India, I co-emceed a large Buddhist festival in Berkeley, California. I was a little anxious. In India, learned about the *theory* of redefining success and failure as one perfect wholeness—but that didn't mean I could always *apply* it.

The Berkeley Buddhist festival was my first time emceeing such an event in a big theater with a lot of attendees, acting as a leader in a religion foreign to me. I love Buddhism, but I'm not a real Buddhist—just Buddhist adjacent. I was hardly an expert, plus I struggled to pronounce the names of many of the Buddhist teachers I was supposed to introduce.

Brian, the co-emcee, and I worked on our opening patter. We planned brief introductions for each speaker. I learned how to say the monks' tongue-twisty names. We also strategized how to keep the program moving if a monk decided to ramble. We arrived at the venue, and I reveled in the joy of working in a large theater again. It was a homecoming on steroids, because not only was I in a theater: I knew my custom-made stage-plus-spiritual experience would help me serve well.

I did serve well—and the bulk of my service was backstage.

In the green room, I comforted monks who had never spoken in public.

"You'll be great," I said. "I have complete confidence in you."

I communicated with the backstage crew, the stage manager, and others ensuring they had what they needed to do their work as unsung heroes. I helped monks learn the ways of theater. When one asked me, "How do I know when to walk onstage?" I replied, "Just stand in the wings and we'll cue you." He said, "Okay…Um… what are the wings?" I took him to the black curtained sides of the stage and taught him how to stand so the crowd wouldn't see him. "You'll want to surprise the audience," I said. "That way, they'll be extra excited to meet you."

On our last day together, the monk who was scheduled to speak next went missing. The stage manager whisper-bellowed at me, "Get on the stage now, and tell jokes until we find him." I couldn't think of one Buddhist-friendly joke. So I ambled onstage and leaned into the microphone. I milked the expectant silence as if I was about to announce the coming of the Dalai Lama, and said, "We seem to be missing a monk. Has anyone seen him? He's got a shaved head and he's wearing a robe." Most everyone there had a shaved head and a robe. In the laughter that ensued, the wandering monk returned, and the conference flowed on.

My time at the Berkeley Buddhist festival shattered another illusion. In the past, I sought the distinction of being seen. I grasped at importance via spotlights and applause. I believed these things would get me the approval I craved—and approval would give my life meaning.

At the Buddhist festival, I unveiled another paradox: There is something more important than personal importance.

The spotlight pales in comparison to the inner light of unseen service. My service behind-the-scenes brought unconditional and immeasurable meaning.

I found deep meaning in quiet preparation; joy in my eager search to find ways to help; blessings in an infinite bow to life; a release from transitory-performance-dependent applause. I could shine by encouraging others to shine. These small acts of unseen service brought something that *felt* like applause—that is, an eternal reverberation of *reverence*. And reverence is a form of *giving* applause to the unstoppable grace of being. Again, giving what we wish to receive changes everything.

Service is not a rehearsal for some future reward. When we are mindful and kind-full—willing to secretly support the greater good without personal accolades—perfection reveals itself in everything we do. Service becomes joy and joy becomes service. The two become one in a never-ending spiral of grace. We find our inner missing monk; then we collectively discover our wings and silently soar out loud.

Reflections

Head: Is there any place in your life where you are grasping for applause, external validation, or other? What might it be like to let that go?

Heart: Divine Love, show me new ways to offer unseen service. Help me release my expectations for future rewards so I may revel in the service of giving now.

Hands: Practice letting go of future rewards. Treat each moment as a perfect, present, unconditional bow to life.

KINDNESS AROUND THE WORLD

"Simple kindness may be the most vital key to the riddle of how human beings can live with each other in peace and care properly for this planet we all share."

—Bo Lozoff

Nipun's message about small acts of kindness continues to inspire the members of our center. He has visited us many times, and many of our members have participated in various ServiceSpace offerings. We carry the message of ServiceSpace via small acts of kindness. The capacity for kindness is omnipresent and infinite in each person. Often, adversity is a catalyst.

If we hear of a hate crime, we send love mail. We fill out postcards addressed to survivors of hateful acts and state, "We love you, we stand by you, and we pray for you."

When someone bombed a Sikh-owned FedEx building in the Midwest, we practiced Vasudhaiva Kutumbakam (the whole world is one family) and offered support to a nearby Sikh Gurdwara. This started a friendship. Jaspreet, the local Sikh Kirtan leader, contacted me to express her gratitude. She told me Sikhs are often targeted because the men wear turbans. People first assume they are Muslim and then assume they are terrorists. She spoke at our church, told us about the beauty of Sikhism, and asked us to spread love and respect for this religion and its followers.

Our local synagogue had their sign defaced by a hate message. Members of our church created paper hearts and posed by the sign holding these hearts. Our purpose was to send two messages to the world: first, that we love our Jewish brothers and sisters; second, that only love will heal hatred.

The Children of Jai Jagat.

We raised funds to bring 17 children and their mentors from an underprivileged area of India to the United States. The children were members of a performance group, Jai Jagat, who created a play about Gandhi, kindness, and bringing love to all.[36] Our joyful

---
36 Jai Jagat, pronounced Jay Juh-gut can be translated as "Victory to the Earth." For more information about the 2019 Jai Jagat Tour go to this website: Empty Hands Music, www.emptyhandsmusic.org.

fundraising allowed us to receive so much more than we gave. Several years after the Jai Jagat troupe's visit, one sweet church member still talks about how meeting the children was one of the most meaningful experiences of her life. "The children bowed and touched my feet," she says. More than that, they touched her soul.

Several teachers in our congregation offer kindness challenges in our local school system to teach children about the power of small acts. The children in our church create plays, film them, and send them to other children in places like Ghana, Nigeria, and Afghanistan. This work was inspired by a ServiceSpace friend, "Fran from Iran," and indirectly encouraged by Janessa, another ServiceSpace friend and former CIA agent who served in Iraq and now has a peace-building organization.[37]

We offered an "encouragement booth" at our local Pride festival and at the Berkeley Buddhist festival. We invited people to sit at our table and color a patterned mandala-like tablecloth. We asked our visitors about their lives. If they spoke of challenges, we asked for permission to encourage them. If they said yes, we shared universally applicable words about a power and presence greater than any difficulty.

When we noticed our kindness was going global, we installed a map of the world in our social hall. We call it a ripple map, as it demonstrates the ripples of good from Ventura circulating globally. We place pins in the spots where we have touched lives. We have pins in Asia, Europe, the Middle East, Africa, Australia, and the Americas. Still no pins in the Arctic Circles, or Saturn—but maybe someday.

One of my personal acts of kindness happened in Jordan. Myron, a friend I met in India, invited me to visit Jordan with

---

[37] "Fran from Iran" is Fran Faraz, the Peace Studies Program Director at Golden West College. www.goldenwestcollege.edu; Janessa Wilder, www.euphratesinstitute.org.

a group that serves Syrian refugees.[38] I said yes, again without knowing why, just a feeling I was supposed to go. Myron has worked with refugees off and on for years. He provided constant support when the Syrian crisis first escalated. By the time I went to Jordan, things had calmed down significantly. My primary role was to work with young medical students. We hoped to offer them communication strategies to help them provide emotional care for traumatized refugees.

The team leader introduced me to seven female students. They were dressed modestly in Hijab, long-sleeved floor length dresses and heads covered. They were kind and polite but seemed a little afraid of me. I'm not sure why. They may have been naturally reserved, but also they may have been aware of the prejudices some Americans hold toward Middle Eastern people, especially Muslims.

We made awkward small talk. Then inspiration struck me. I was a retired nurse. I could speak with them about disgusting medical issues—one of my favorite topics.

"How do you say 'fever' in Arabic?" I asked.

They told me. I repeated it, and they gently laughed at my pronunciation.

Then I said, "How about 'coma'?"

Again, they told me, I said it, and they laughed louder, gaining trust.

We went back and forth with a few words. There was a moment of satisfied silence, as we all pondered the magic of this exchange. Suddenly, one Syrian woman came out of her reverie, smiled brightly, and said, "I know! Let's try 'vomit'!"

We all laughed together as they taught me the Arabic word for "vomit," which to me sounded a bit guttural—kind of like

---

38 Shamanic Teacher, Ancestral Healer | Myron Eshowsky

you might throw up in your mouth when you say it. I shared my observation with the medical students, and with more laughter, they agreed.

This went on for days. We started with basic symptoms—your fever, your coma, your vomit. Eventually, as we became friends, we worked ourselves up to more intense conditions—your mucous, your maggots, and your anal fistulas. Good times.

By the end of my stay in Jordan, these Middle Eastern women who once seemed intimidated by me, now actively sought me out. I was their new American friend. Every day I walked into the lunchroom, wondering where I should sit. When these young women spotted me, an American old lady with a juvenile sense of humor, they vigorously waved me over to their table to join. We ate lunch, bonded, and laughed at the strange comedy embedded in medical anomalies.

Then I learned more about them—their dress, their music, how they liked to dance, and their religious practices. I discovered how eager they were to have Americans think well of them. They asked me to take a picture of them studying so I could show my friends in America they were not stereotypes of oppressed Middle Eastern women. They freely explored science, art, spirituality, and fun. I filmed one woman who spoke to me about the Islamic prayer ritual that devout Muslims offer five times a day. She shared how she checks in with Allah for guidance and how she asks for forgiveness each time. She, too, asked me to share this information with other Americans.

I cherished the whole experience and asked God again, *How did you know to put me there? It seems an uncanny combination—a former nurse, with an operatic love of language, and a medical vocabulary teaming up with young medical students in the Middle East. How did you think that up, God? And what a blessing it was to converge with new friends, people who are just like me, with a range of interests spanning global friendships to music to anal fistulas. God, you are amazing!*

I have forgotten all the medical Arabic I learned from my new friends (except for vomit—I can still say that and barf a little as I do). It doesn't matter that I've forgotten the specifics, because I remember the treasures found in the exchange. The warmth, the joy, the laughter. The grace of people from different cultures drawn together by curiosity and friendship. I don't know if we did anything to cement American and Middle East relations. I don't think we solved centuries-worth of bigotry and discord. But we did something.

Medical Students in Jordan.

We invited conscious awareness of the bonds we share beyond language, beyond culture, beyond bias, or dress code. Every culture shares medical anomalies. We started there and then moved to joy. Joy in the vicissitudes of being human. Joy in forging friendship with the alleged other—and joy in God's stunning ability to move us into surprising service.

Reflections

Head: Where do you experience "the other?" Is there a way you can find something in common?

Heart: Divine Love, inspire me to share my heart with our global family. Help me find unique ways to build trust and empathy.

Hands: Actively seek out "the other" and explore a common interest, no matter how trivial it may seem to be.

COMPASSION CONSCIOUSNESS

"It is easy enough to be friendly to one's friends. But to befriend the one who regards himself as your enemy is the quintessence of true religion."

—Mahatma Gandhi

In the prologue of this story, I mentioned many see heaven as a destination—a place where we get to go if we have believed and behaved. My faith teaches that heaven and hell are states of mind, experienced in the omnipresent now. We *can* call forth heaven on earth—but *do* we?

Sometimes in metaphysical teachings, we have a narrow definition of what heaven on earth looks like. We pray to get what we want. If we get it, we're in heaven. If we don't get what we want, we act as if we're in hell. It's fine to pray for what we want. We are here to express creatively and sometimes our creative urges inspire specific manifestations. But it's also important to remember love is unconditional. Because we are love in human form, we are called to be unconditional. In other words, if we don't get exactly what we want, when we want it, we don't have to live in mental hell. Love is bigger than that.

The COVID-19 pandemic entered our lives in 2020. We shut down the church and went to online streaming services produced by a small team of loyal volunteers. I mentioned before how the pandemic had an impact on church life. Attendance and income dropped; our board president called me a prostitute when I devised a marketing plan; and we wondered if the church would survive. The church did survive and today we are rebuilding, reinventing, and moving toward thriving. We anticipate our reinvention will continue to evolve according to divine will, at the speed of love. It couldn't be any other way.

The pandemic brought stress and strain, but also offered many gifts. One gift was a revisit to the idea that "we create our illnesses." This notion, cherished in many metaphysical teachings, often plagues spiritual seekers. My congregation tells me years ago, church members stayed away from Sunday services if they received an unfortunate diagnosis. They were ashamed, wondering if people would judge them and say, "How did you create your illness?" or, "Sorry you have cancer consciousness."

My heart aches for the people who feel they must protect themselves from the judgment of others at times when they need support. I wonder, *How did we stray from loving ourselves and one another? When did we get so judgmental about the human condition? How can it be appropriate to treat illnesses or those who have illnesses like our enemies?*

I began questioning the idea of creating our own illnesses years ago when our church office assistant's cat developed a problem in his little testicles. Kristin, the cat-mom, asked me to find a metaphysical website that identifies mental causes of illnesses. When I consulted the internet, I found a site that offered a list of specific thoughts that could create rancid testicles. The site suggested an affirmation to change one's thinking about testes. According to this source, the cat had masculinity issues.

He was supposed to affirm, "I am at peace with being a man." Kristin the cat mom and I laughed as we said the affirmation over and over again on behalf of the kitty. Then Kristin took the cat to the vet. The vet chopped off the wicked testicles and the kitty got better.

Then during the pandemic, I thought I caught COVID. Granted, it wasn't as serious as coming down with the cancer I had in the past. It wasn't as bad as the besmirched gonads of Kristin's cat. But some lapse in spiritual sanity inspired me to join an inner chorus of quiet judgers. I worried, *Bonnie, what if you have COVID consciousness?*

It was only a mild case of disease-shaming. Still, even with all the work I've done on releasing judgment around "prayer-fails," I didn't want my congregation to know. I knew if I had COVID, I was required to tell them and wondered if they would judge me: *Reverend Bonnie has COVID consciousness. She probably did something wrong.* And I didn't "do something wrong." I built my faith in well-being. I wore my mask, got my vaccines, stood six feet away from people at the grocery store, and sang *The Doxology* while washing my hands. I wasn't terribly afraid of catching COVID. But I did all of these things as a former nurse who understands disease transmission. I did these things to respect others and keep them safe.

While I waited for test results, I probed my heart and mind. I decided to heal the lingering judgment around "we create our illnesses" once and for all. If I healed it for me, I could offer healing wisdom to every disease-shamer in my denomination and beyond.

During the possible COVID, I felt like crap—fever, body aches, and no energy. My depleted energy gave me more time to meditate. After several sessions of contemplating my alleged

"COVID consciousness," I began to hear astounding spiritual prophecies such as, "So what?" "Who cares?" and "No big deal."

If I had COVID consciousness, it would only siphon my esteem to the extent that I attacked myself with it. So I used my brand of finding sweetness in the human condition. I witnessed and befriended possible COVID consciousness. I examined my thoughts from the perspective of kindness. I welcomed feelings as they arose and looked at how they could inspire me to align with greater love.

I wondered, *How judgmental would you like to be today? You know it's a choice, right?* I concluded if I attacked myself for having COVID, my judgment made a harsh statement about the millions of people who had been caught by the virus. When I saw how unkind it was to accuse others of COVID consciousness, it seemed logical to stop accusing myself.

This idea of judging others as a form of self-judgment mirrors Jesus's teachings on love. Love your neighbor as you love yourself is often translated, "love your neighbor *as much as* you love yourself."[vii] It's far more literal than that. As you love yourself, you simultaneously love your neighbor. As you love your neighbor, you love yourself, because *we are all one being*. We forget the same law applies to judgment. As you judge your neighbor, you judge yourself, and vice versa. "Your judgment judges you," as Ernest Holmes says.

With this in mind, I scaled back the judgment of myself and others. I didn't need to let the judgment take root. The judgment didn't need to become the evil plant in *Little Shop of Horrors* that grows huge and spreads itself in a rampage of destruction. Without fertilizer, my judgment wilted into the nothingness of illusion. The lack of judgment created a void that "left some room for the Holy Spirit," a place where miracles and new insights could flourish.

I thought about all of the beings, businesses, families, and health care workers suffering in the onslaught of the pandemic. I saw how people felt helpless as they wrestled with uncertainty and how they so often looked for someone to blame. I thought about my vet's office and the DMV with their signs begging people to be kind. I remembered a global prayer call for India we did with ServiceSpace. The second wave of the pandemic hit India hard. It destroyed families and severely impacted the food supply chain. People from all over the world gathered and prayed for our extended global family.

As I reflected on the trajectory of the pandemic, I saw profound meanings far beyond my petty thoughts about creating our own illnesses. So I prayed my Buddhist-adjacent version of Metta, a loving-kindness meditation. "May you be safe, may you be healthy, may you be happy, may you be peaceful and at ease." I prayed this for all beings and the whole world. It felt good to pray. "Excellent," I said. "If I have COVID consciousness, bring it on. I am grateful for a deeper understanding of my brothers and sisters. I am grateful to participate in the suffering *and* the solution."

The word compassion means "to suffer with." Once again, suffering became joy. And COVID consciousness became compassion consciousness.

As it turned out, I didn't have COVID. The cause of my symptoms was probably an unfortunate encounter with canned stuffed grape leaves. They smelled a little bit like our compost bin, but I ate them anyway. I guess I had compost consciousness.

I don't regret it. I don't regret the fever, the body aches, the lethargy, or the self-accusation. I don't regret the possible COVID, or the possible food poisoning. I don't regret the compost consciousness. Because just as I got busy with fear and judgment, just as I assumed the position for inadequacy, God offered me an opportunity to learn a better way. God's way affirmed universal oneness. There I found the compassion consciousness that will serve many in years to come.

From now on, if anyone ever accuses themselves of creating an illness through faulty thoughts, I'll suggest a new approach. "Maybe you don't have disease consciousness. Maybe God is calling you to embrace compassion consciousness. Let's enjoy it. Let's embrace compassion consciousness together, right now. Let us pray for the well-being of the cosmos."

And if the person still needs a reason "why," I'll say, "Because everything exists to call us to greater love."

Reflections

Head: Have you ever disease-shamed yourself or others? Are you willing to change that? Ask yourself, "How judgmental would you like to be today?"

Heart: Divine Love, teach me to use everything as a portal to compassion consciousness.

Hands: As you go about your day, silently repeat "compassion consciousness" to yourself. Does this simple phrase help you move through life differently?

EPILOGUE: THE CIRCLE GAME

*"There are love dogs no one knows the names of.
Give your life to be one of them."*

—Rumi

When I was around 10 years old, my sister, Nancy, became a hippy. She wore tie-dyed shirts, bell bottoms, and fist-sized gold hoop earrings. Nancy had an immense multi-colored peace sign painted on the wall of her apartment in Florida. She also played the guitar, and we sang songs together. One of the songs we sang was *The Circle Game,* by Joni Mitchell.

When I first started singing professionally, I worked with a guitarist who played Joni Mitchell's music. I learned most of Joni's songs and sang them in coffee houses and on the lawn of the Duke University Medical School for an afternoon concert. I also listened to Joni Mitchell LPs with Debbie, my Vizsla-loving friend who persuaded us to fall in love with Stella.

Now, 40 years later, I prepared to sing a Joni Mitchell song in public for the first time in ages. I planned to dedicate the song to Debbie, who died suddenly a few weeks before my second trip to India.

My pipes were a little rusty. I was underdressed, wearing my infamous pink hoodie to stay warm, but it was a casual event, so that was okay. Many of the people in the audience probably didn't know of Joni Mitchell. Many were young and many didn't speak English. None of it mattered. None of it marred the perfection of the moment.

My friend, Nimo Patel, a South Asian rapper/humanitarian leader, asked me to sing in this concert.[39] We were in Jordan, seven miles from the Syrian border. The stage was set up in a park, high off the ground with piles of heavy black sound equipment. There weren't many people there, maybe 75 at the most, but it was a diverse group.

I looked out at the audience and saw the Hijab-clad medical students, my new friends who taught me how to say "vomit" in Arabic. The male medical students were there, too, as kind and charming as their female counterparts. To the left, a group of young German social workers stood huddled together. It was chilly and they linked arms to stay warm. The "German girls," as I called them, sang Christmas carols in German with me when we traveled in busses and cars to our various destinations in Jordan.

The rest of the concert attendees were families, mothers, fathers, and lots of children, presumably Syrian refugees. There were two men dressed in clown costumes. I saw my colleagues who served with me in Jordan, a psychiatrist, a shaman, a doctor, more social workers, a writer, and a few psychologists.

This was another moment when time stopped and I asked, *Why me God? What did I do to deserve this moment? I never imagined my life would turn out this way. And even if I had, God, I never could have planned it with your exquisite artistry. How did I arrive seven miles from the Syrian border to sing a song that has followed me my whole life? Who put these puzzle pieces together?*

---

39 Nimo Patel, www.emptyhandsmusic.org.

I thought back to a time with Stella a few days before she died. My friends who work in pet bereavement told me I should I make an impression of her paw "while she was still living." They insisted getting a footprint from a living dog was essential.

I drove to an art supply store where I sought out the pet section and found a product called The Pet Memorial Steppingstone. The picture on the box showed a well-behaved golden retriever daintily stepping in wet cement. The box promised I could get a pristine concrete paw print of my pet. Then I could decorate the stone with mosaic tiles. I was skeptical, so I bought two.

I arrived home, mixed the concrete, and began the task of convincing Stella to step in it. After she spent days of languishing, almost too weak to walk, I thought it would be easy. But Stella took one look at the wet cement and surged through the doggie door. She snaked around the fruit trees in our back yard, avoiding me as I chirped and coaxed from behind with my vat of solidifying goo. The first batch hardened before I corralled her.

Batch number two was a stealth endeavor. I mixed it in secret, held it behind my back, and snuck up behind Stella. I straddled her and aimed the wet cement at her paw. Once again, my dying dog rallied. Her willfulness surpassed my skillfulness. She pushed and struggled against my intention to preserve her memory. The result looked like a crater on the rough grey surface of the moon. In deference to Stella's last wishes, I gave up. She had no interest in creating a cherished keepsake. There would be no footprint for me.

A few days later, Stella died peacefully in my arms. Hugh and I drove her to the vet for cremation. We stroked her everywhere, smelled her ears, and held her paws. I wished I had a footprint, but I didn't. I sighed and said good-bye.

A week later a card arrived at my home. Two veterinary techs, Meghan and Josie, copied the Rainbow Bridge poem and fastened it to a piece of construction paper. To the left of the poem was a small patch of Stella's red fur. At the bottom right, there was an ink footprint. Stella's footprint.

I stood in my living room, touched the footprint, and wept. I looked at the card for days afterwards. Something about it slayed me with tears and hope. I thought, *Is this just a card, or is it perfectly-timed love? Are Meghan and Josie Bodhisattvas? Are they awakened beings who devote themselves to reconciling the suffering of others by finding and serving what matters most? And what does matter most?*

Love, of course. Earlier I asked *who puts the puzzle pieces of our lives together?* The answer has to be love. Love is the process and the prize. Love is the journey and the destination. Love is the rehearsal and the performance. Love is in every epic drama and every tiny detail.

My whole life, I've been carried by something bigger than me. It was love. Love offered me a fantastic family, where I learned about dying moms and dogs who vomit on your Amy Vanderbilt book of etiquette. Love gave me Bessie the Skel, who perhaps sparked an early interest in medicine and osteo-anatomy. Love sent me to nursing school where I learned disgusting medical terms that would later translate into relationships with young Muslim women. Love sent me to music school where I experienced the treasures of opera so I could sing a song about death as I ricocheted through the traffic in India. Love introduced me to my husband by the fountain in front of Lincoln Center. Love brought me a cat, then another cat, and then sent us on a Broadway tour. Love moved us to California, where Debbie and Jeff loved us into life with dogs.

Stella's love changed our lives and pointed me to my church. Love created challenges in the church that grew my soul. Love created a sacred story with my congregation so we could blossom into something subtly magnificent. Love made a spiritual celebrity refuse my advances so we could find Nipun and ServiceSpace. Love brought me to Jordan to sing a song about love. Only love could orchestrate the synchronicities of an ordinary, yet splendid life.

I started this story with a verse from the Gospel of Thomas: "The kingdom of heaven is spread upon the earth, but we do not see it." When you look back on your life and look at all that conspired to make you who you are today, can you see heaven's footprints at work? Can you see love acting through everything, in the failures, triumphs, sorrows, and joys? I can. And I hope you can, too. But if you can't, I'll see the absolute truth of love's omni-presence in your life for you. For I know love is everything; love is your whole life; and your whole life loves you more than you can imagine.

Back to the concert in Jordan: Nimo the humanitarian rapper called me onto the stage. He introduced me and asked me to sing. There, under the sparkling stars, amidst a crowd of new friends, love sang the truth through me:

And the seasons, they go round and round.
And the painted ponies go up and down.
We're captive on a carousel of time.
We can't return, we can only look behind from where we came,
And go round, and round, and round in the circle game.

"The kingdom of heaven is spread upon the earth." Let us dwell in it together as one, always. Namaste.

Heart Pins made by the women of India. Photo by Jennifer Luce.

ACKNOWLEDGEMENTS

I'll be honest—writing this book scared me. Between my sometimes-spicy language, weird sense of humor, and a fixation on my own personal shortcomings, I felt shy about sharing my story with others. "This book could get me in trouble," I told myself—and anyone else who would listen.

Fortunately, I encountered several entities who chose to ignore my inner drama.

First, there's God: Divine Love whispered in my ear, saying "Authenticity is more important than safety." Then the mystical poet Rumi echoed the Divine by telling me, *"Live where you fear to live. Destroy your reputation. Be notorious."*

Okay, I'll give that a whirl, I thought. *Let me share my story with a few trusted others, just to test the waters.*

There was my amazing editor, Alicia Doyle, a former champion boxer, journalist, and now an author. Alicia, I wouldn't have written this book without your encouragement. Thank you for your expert editing and guidance. Thank you for preserving my voice as a writer. Thank you for not using any of your wild boxing moves on me, when you felt it necessary to reign me in. There was no verbal punching with you, only gentle nudges.

My early readers and proofreaders—Becky Burnham, Brock Travis, Chris Kimbler, Annette Bennett, Hugh A. Rose, and Amy

Michelson. Brian Ehler who updated my photos, gave me tech support when needed; and Shelly Ehler who literally hypnotized me to alleviate writers' anxiety. Thank you all for loving me and my story. You gave me the confidence to keep going, when procrastination threatened to overtake me, when the writing felt tedious and futile.

My beautiful sisters, Judy, Nancy, and Carol; plus my parents John and Emily. Thank you for your support both then and now. Thank you for sharing an amazing childhood with me—a time when we were raised with wit, wisdom, love, and *a lot* of music. You will always be the people who help me remember where I came from and who I am.

My amazing church—your dedication, your willingness to teach and learn, your faith in co-creating a Center of Love in a tumultuous world, your patience with me, especially at the beginning when I had no idea how to serve from the heart. I am the luckiest minister in the world because of you. The practitioners, the board, the staff, the volunteers, the community—you are all a blessing beyond measure. I hope this book encourages you as much as you have encouraged me. I am so grateful for each of you.

Big thanks to Nipun Mehta and all my friends at ServiceSpace for inspiring me to explore a radical, counter-intuitive way of being "in the world but not of the world." Thank you for teaching me the priceless values of kindness and inner transformation. Thank you for establishing a place for me in your global family. I will never underestimate the mystical forces that conspired to bring us together and the intangible treasures you have offered to me, my church family, and beyond. You all are other-worldly amazing.

Thank you to Lonnie Cassidy for being who you are: a "tell-it-like-it-is" yet encouraging board president, friend, and fellow animal lover. Thank you, Deana, for sharing your poignant story.

Thank you to Jose Ramirez of Pedernales Publishing and Eric Labacz, our cover designer. The kind guidance you both provided was exceptional.

A big thank you to every animal companion who has ever shared my life. A big thank you to those who love and serve animals. And the biggest thank you of all goes to my husband, Hugh. Your love, encouragement, companionship, loyalty, skill as an actor/writer, and your spiritual wisdom has blessed me and will bless me forever.

For everyone I didn't mention—please know how important you are to me. Thank you for being who you are. I love you all.

— Bonnie

ENDNOTES

[i] Cynthia Bourgeault, *The Wisdom Jesus, Transforming Heart and Mind—a New Perspective on Christ and His Message* (Boston: Shambala Press, 2008), pp. 33-35.

[ii] Ernest Holmes, *What We Believe: The "Declaration of Principles* that first appeared in *Science of Mind Magazine*, 1927.

[iii] Thornton Wilder, *Our Town*. (Harper Perennial, 2003, originally published in 1938).

[iv] Joel Goldsmith, *A Parentheses in Eternity—Living the Mystical Life* (San Francsiso: Harper, 1986). Title.

[v] David Sedaris. *A Plague of Tics*, in *Naked*. (New York, Boston, London. Little, Brown, and Company: Back Bay Books, 1997). pp. 13-26.

[vi] Wayne Muller. *A Life of Being, Having, and Doing Enough* (New York: Three Rivers Press, 2010, p. 132

[vii] Cynthia Bourgeault, *The Wisdom Jesus*, page 42.